SETTING THE CAPTIVES FREE
THUR
DELIVERANCE

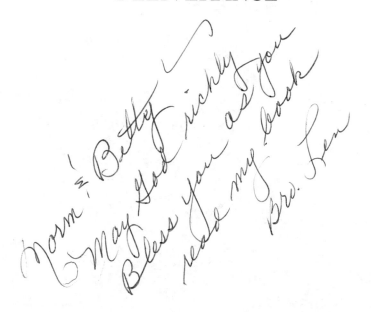

Norm & Betty
May God richly
Bless you as you
read my book
Bro. Len

Len Ward

SETTING THE CAPTIVES FREE
THUR
DELIVERANCE

Len Ward

A Christian Voice Publishing

ISBN:1934327123

Unless otherwise referenced, all scripture in taken from the King
James Bible. Some scripture references are partial.

Cover Design:
Amy Poster
Superior, WI

Scott Peterson
Duluth, MN 55806

Published by
A Christian Voice Publishing
102 S. 29th Ave. W.
Suite 103
Duluth, MN 55806

Preface

What are the advantages of following the discipleship plan of Jesus Christ? There's a story that when Jesus was taken up the heaven the angel asked him if he succeeded of what he came to earth for. Jesus informed the angel of his discipleship plan. The angel replied: What if it doesn't work! Jesus said, "I have no other plan."

I guess if you would ask me why I decided to write a book I'd probably say it was out of frustration. The mind-set of Christianity in general is not where the Lord would like it to be. When the Israelites crossed the Red Sea out of bondage God spoke to them and said (Ex 15:3). "The Lord is a man of war!" That hasn't changed! That war is still going on but you wouldn't know it by some of the mindset that is in the Christian circles today! Power is needed to win a war but there is very little emphasis on the Baptism in the Holy Spirit and almost none on deliverance.

It is my desire that this book will open up our understanding of the spiritual realm. God has not changed, so it must be us! Where are we lacking, what is the reason?

Satan has deceived the Church! The main deception is that we have not looked to Jesus, the author and finisher of our faith. God told his disciples at the transfiguration "This is my son hear ye him!" Matt 17:2-5

Jesus was present when Adam sinned. He witnessed the depravity of man. He saw the results, people were suffering in many different ways. His discipleship program is designed to redeem that what was lost. (The intimacy with God).

The main deception is our inability to recognize that a Christian can have demonic problems and in need of deliverance.

Our lack of taking authority is a big deception! Demonic powers will not move unless pressure is used! It is asked how can a believer who is filled with the Holy Ghost, able to speak in tongues have any demonic spirits? I answer that question in my book!

I was delivered of diabetes. I attended a "Deliverance seminar" by David Middleton, in Duluth, Minnesota a few years ago and I purchased a tape "casting out demon spirits of diabetes" over a period of time my readings started coming down. I've had normal readings ever since.

In this book you will find that almost everyone whom Jesus delivered of evil spirits were believers, even the Gadarene demoniac. John 14:12 Jesus: The works that I do you will do! It's like Jesus is handing His believers "The baton to finish the race" doing the same things! God's blessings on you as you read!

John 3:3 Jesus: **Prayer of Salvation**

Ye must be born again!
Dear God, I've been living my life my own way. Now I want to live my life your way. I need you and I am now willing for you to take control of my life. I receive your Son Jesus Christ, as my personal Savior and Lord. I believe He died for my sins and has risen from the dead. I surrender to Him as Lord. Jesus, make me the kind of person you want me to be, Amen

About the Author

Len Ward is 79 years old, a retired fireman from Superior, Wisconsin, he worked 36 years on the fire dept. working his way up to the position of assistant chief.

Len was married to his wife Ernestine for 59 years until she passed away in 2005. He has 3 children, 5 grandchildren and 6 great-grandchildren. He has been walking with the Lord for 43 years. Involved in spiritual warfare for many years with the emphasis on setting the captives free.

Thru the years Len was an early riser spending his time with the Lord. The Lord started giving him material and he would put it on the shelf. Time went on and it was very clear that spiritual warfare was the main topic.

The Lord gave Len a burden to help those Christians that are having difficulties in finding joy in their lives. Many Christians are slaves to addictions, are held in bondage because of curses, evil soul-ties, and the lack of God's Word being used in their lives. Len's ministry is based on the last words of Jesus Christ.

"Go and make disciples!"

TABLE OF CONTENTS

Chapter One

Deliverance

What is deliverance?

Deliverance is the casting out of demons, out of the human body.

The word "Deliverance comes from the verb deliver according to the dictionary means to loose, untie, unbind, release, liberate, set free, redeem.

The ministry of deliverance from evil spirits is a scriptural & much needed ministry for today! This book is for Christians. The word of God states "the enemy will come in like a flood and the standard that will be raised against him will be discipleship with deliverance."

Every believer needs a certain measure of deliverance, because of the sins of our forefathers. There are curses that go back 3rd and 4th generations. "Lam 5:7 our fathers have sinned and are not and we have borne their iniquities.

In my family tree there was a curse of diabetes. My grandmother had it, she died from it, had her foot cut off. My two brothers have diabetes, my oldest son has it. I broke the curse and cast out the evil spirit of diabetes, it took awhile though. John 14:12 Jesus said the works that I do you will do.

It's like running a relay race when you pass the baton to the next person he continues the same way. Jesus has passed the baton to us. Mark 16:17 Jesus: these signs shall follow those who believe. They shall cast out Devils!

I wonder why Jesus made the statement in Matt 6:33... seek ye 1st the kingdom of God.

It must be important!

Jesus preached it. Luke 4:43 I must preach the kingdom of God to the other cities also.

Luke 4:41…Demon spirits came out of the many. Paul preached it Acts 20:25 The kingdom of God Act 20:27 "I have not shunned to declare unto you "the full counsel of God!" Kingdom of God is the full counsel of God! Philip preached the Kingdom of God" Acts 8:12 for unclean spirits came out of many!

Matt 12:28…When you cast out evil spirits the kingdom of God has come upon you.

How can a Christian have a Demon? How can the Holy Spirit and Evil spirits live in the same Body?

Man is a triune being he's made up of 3 parts

1. Spirit= intuition – worship – conscience
2. Soul = mind- will – emotions
3. Body= bones- flesh- blood

When a person receives Christ as savoir his spirit is activated. It was dead (result of Adam's fall)

Eph 2:1 We were dead in trespasses and sins. Note! We weren't dead in our soul (mind-will-emotions) nor our Body (Bones-flesh-blood) we were dead in our spirit, our soul and body are fragmented and demonized! Eph. 2:22 we have a habitation with God "In the spirit" Our body is the house of the Holy Spirit.

Rom. 8:10 If Christ be in you the body is dead because of sin but the spirit is life because of righteousness!

Rom 8:16 The spirit itself bears witness with our spirit that "we are the children of God!"

The big discussion against deliverance is it is the flesh we have to contend with. Well if it's the flesh then it will be healed thru prayer.

Note! The boil on the back of my neck will not heal until the core comes out!

Important references for Deliverance:

Deliverance

A Bonified Ministry of Jesus Christ?

Almost anywhere you go in the spiritual world you will not find the ministry of Jesus Christ, casting out devils. As you look at the word of God you'll find that there is almost as many accounts of His casting out evil spirits as there are of healing the sick.

In fact in each of the four gospels approximately 53 accounts of healing are mentioned with a total of about 256 verses. At the same time, approximately 38 separate accounts are written of Christ's ministry of deliverance, for a total of about 219 verses. By comparing these two figures, you'll find a scant 15% greater emphasis on Jesus' healing ministry than on His ministry of casting out demon spirits. Yet, we don't find even a 15% emphasis on this ministry?

Mark 16:17: (Jesus) These signs shall follow those that believe, 1st they shall cast out devils, 2nd they shall speak with new tongues, 3rd they shall lay hands on the sick.

It is unscriptural even to preach the gospel without including the message of deliverance. In the gospels, each time Jesus gave the commission to believers, three things are common. These are preaching, casting out evil spirits and healing. The early Church was faithful to execute "all three" parts of the commission. (They were a powerful Church!)

In reading (Mark 3:22-30) we find when Jesus was accused of casting out demons by the prince of demons, Jesus stated that to relagate this ministry to anything other than the Holy Spirit is an unforgivable sin!

Jesus' ministry of deliverance was to believers.

1. Luke 13:16: The woman with the spirit of infirmity.
2. Mark 5:6: The Gaderene demoniac.
3. Matthew 15:22-28: The Canaanite women's daughter.
4. Acts 8:3-12 Philip preached Jesus
5. Matthew 16:23 Get thee behind me satan. (Peter)

Cases of Deliverance Ministry of Jesus Christ

I Thessalonians 5:21…Prove all things, hold fast to that which is good!

We as Christians are instructed to prove all things, especially the parts of scripture that would cause some controversy. The rule of the thumb in Christiandom is to prove scripture thru the Strong's concordance. Using the King James Version I was able to prove that the people whom Jesus ministered deliverance to, were believers.

The case of the woman with the spirit of infirmity

Luke 13:10: Jesus was in church teaching and in Church there was a woman   with a "Spirit of infirmity."

Luke 13:13: Jesus laid hands on her and immediately she was made straight and glorified God. Jesus: woman, be loosed from thine infirmity!

Luke 13:16: This woman was a "Daughter of Abraham."

Galatians 3:7: Know ye therefore that they which are of faith, the same are the children of Abraham.

Galatians 3:29: And if ye be Christ's, then ye are Abraham's seed and heirs according to the promise.

II Corinthians 11:22: Paul asked "are they the seed of Abraham? So am I."

The case of the Gadarene demoniac

1. The case of the Gadarene demoniac.
   Mark 5:6: But when he <u>saw</u> Jesus afar off, he <u>ran</u> to Him and "<u>worshipped Him</u>".

2. Was the Gadarene a believer?

3. You will notice that the sinner's prayer is not found in the Bible. "The woman at the well" did not say the sinner's prayer nor did the "Thief on the cross."

4. Romans 10:13: Whosoever shall call upon the name of the Lord shall be saved. Romans 10:9: If thou shalt confess with they mouth the Lord Jesus. And shall believe in thine heart that God raised Him from the dead, thou shalt be saved.

5. The Gadarene demoniac exercised the small amount of will that he had. The word states: <u>he saw</u> Jesus coming out of the boat- <u>he ran</u> to Jesus-<u>he worshipped</u> Jesus! (this man believed and then was delivered). In the Strong's concordance the word "worshipped" is the same word for worship found in Hebrews 1:6 "Let all the angels of God worship Him!"

   Strong's concordance=worship 4352 Worship=reverence to, adore. Webster's dictionary-to adore, to pay divine honors to, to reverence with supreme respect veneration as to worship God.

   Confirmation:
   Mark 5:15: The Gadarene was fully clothed sitting at Jesus' feet.
   Mark 5:18: The Gadarene wanted to go aboard with Jesus.
   Mark 5:19: Jesus said: Go home and tell your friends. <u>He was a believer.</u>

Philip
Acts 8:3-8

At this time there was great persecution against the Church.

Stephen had just been stoned to death and with great mourning they buried him.

Saul was running wild entering the homes of Christians and committing them to prison.

The Church scattered and Philip went to Samaria and preached Christ to them (Acts 8:5)

The people were in one accord (in agreement) of those things that Philip spoke. (Acts 8:6) what things? Jesus Christ! They were believers.

They saw the miracles which Phillip did. For unclean spirits were cast out of many.

Confirmation: Acts 8:8: There was "Great Joy" there! Heathen don't have joy over the works of Jesus. They were Christians!

Canaanite women's daughter
Matthew 15:22-28

Matthew 15:22: O Lord, thou son of David, my daughter is grievously vexed with a devil.

Matthew 15:25: Then she came and worshipped him, saying "Lord, help me!" (The word worship is the same found in Hebrews 1:6) The angels worshipped the Lord!

Matthew 15:26: Then Jesus said: O woman, Great is thy faith, be it unto thee even as thou wilt and her daughter was made whole that very hour. (This mothers needs were met). Faith: reliance upon Jesus Christ for salvation. Strong's concordance 4102 (conviction) of religious truth.

Worship: Webster's dictionary, to reverence with supreme respect.
Worshipped: Strong's concordance 4352: Do reverence to, adore.

Peter
Matthew 16:23

Matthew 16:21: Jesus told His disciples how He must go to Jerusalem and suffer many things, and be killed and raised the third day.

Matthew 16:22: Then Peter rebuked Him saying heaven forbid this is not going to happen to you.

Matthew 16:23: But Jesus turned and said unto Peter "Get thee behind me Satan!"

Matthew 16:19: This happened just after Jesus told Peter about the "Keys of the Kingdom."

Matthew 10:1: Peter was a called disciple of Jesus' twelve.

Mark 16:17, 18: These signs shall follow them that believe, they shall cast out devils, they shall speak with new tongues, they shall lay hands on the sick, and they shall recover.

John 14:12: (Jesus) verily, verily, I say unto you, He that believeth on me, the works that I do ye shall do also.

Is Deliverance for the Church Today?

There has been great controversy in the Christian realm as to whether a Christian can be demonized. In this session we will take a look at some scripture to reveal to us some light on the subject. Be open to the Lord, have a good attitude, ask Him to open your understanding. A good "rule of the thumb" is to pray "Lord, if this is of you then I want it."

Proverbs 28:5 *"They that seek the Lord shall understand all things."* Jesus was always bent on building up the Church, giving them power. The early Church was strong because they ministered in deliverance for the Christian (there were signs and wonders). Mark 16:17, Jesus said *"These signs shall follow them that believe. In my name they shall cast out devils."* The Church is the extension of the ministry of Jesus Christ!

John 14:12, Jesus said *"The works that I do, ye shall do also."* (He was speaking to Christians). With deliverance comes the healing of the soul, as the soul is restored, the joy of the Lord comes. Liberty is experienced as bondages are broken. That is the purpose of discipleship. John 8:31-32, Jesus said, *"If ye continue in my word, then ye are my disciples indeed, ye shall know the truth and the truth shall set you free."*

I Thessalonians 5:23, Paul prayed that your "whole" spirit, soul and body be blameless unto the coming of the Lord Jesus Christ. Man is made up of a spirit, a soul and a body. When a person receives Jesus Christ as savior, His spirit is activated. I Corinthians 6:17, we are joined together with God "In the Spirit." Ephesians 2:22, A Christian's spirit is the habitation of God. Ephesians 2:1, you hath He quickened who were dead in trespasses and sins. John 3:6, Jesus told Nicodemus, what is born of the flesh is flesh and what is born of the spirit is spirit.

Note! A Christian cannot be "demon possessed." To possess means ownership and complete control of. Nothing touches the born-again spirit. The soul which is the (mind-will and emotions) and the body (bones, flesh and the blood) are nesting place for demon spirits.

9

Note! Not in the spirit! The study of the "fragmented soul" will bear this out, God's plan is that through (deliverance) the Church will become progressively healthy. Slowly but surely the enemy will be driven out.

Exodus 23:27-30, Joshua taking of the "Promised land" is a similitude of the winning back the soul and the body. The enemy will be driven out "Little by little!"

The question comes up, is it wise to cast evil spirits out of an unsaved person? It probably can be done in the name of Jesus but what happens after that is where the danger lies. God's word states that if the space vacated by an evil spirit is not filled, he will come back with seven evil spirits more wicked than himself and the last state of that man is worst than the first.

Deliverance, Restoration of the whole man

1. God wants to sanctify you completely
I Thessalonians 5:23, and the very God of peace sanctify you <u>Wholly</u> and I pray your <u>whole</u> spirit, your <u>whole</u> soul and your <u>whole</u> body be preserved <u>blameless</u> unto the coming of our Lord Jesus Christ.

2. Jesus 1ˢᵗ Sermon
Luke 4:18…Preach the gospel to the poor, heal the broken hearted, preach deliverance to the captives, recovering the sight of the blind, set at liberty them that are bruised.

3. Salvation-an ongoing process
Philippians 2:12, Work out your own <u>salvation</u> with fear and trembling. <u>Salvation</u> Thayer's Lexicon "soteria" means deliverance from bondages.

4. Salvation to the uttermost
Hebrew 7:25…Wherefore He is able to save them to the uttermost. Save 4982 Strong's concordance=5020-to deliver, to make whole. Uttermost-3838 Strong's concordance= full, completion, entire.

5. Blasphemy against the Holy Ghost
Matthew 12:28…If I cast out devils by the spirit of God, then the kingdom of God is come unto you. All manner of sin and blasphemy will be forgiven, but the blasphemy against the Holy Ghost will not be forgiven. (Matthew 12:31) (Mark 3:29).

The Thrust of Jesus' ministry: drive out the old nature—take on the new.

The Nature of Demons
What are Demons like in Character?

They are just like the devil in most ways and in other ways much like people. The following are some of their personality characteristics.

1. **Demons possess knowledge.**
   Mark 1:24: The demon in the man in the synagogue said to Jesus "I know who you are, the holy one of God."

2. **Demons possess a will.**
   Matthew 12:44: The unclean spirit who has gone out of a man, but can find no place to rest says "I will return into my house from whence I came out."

3. **Demons have strong emotions.**
   Acts 8:7: For unclean spirits crying with a loud voice came out of many.

4. **Demons have degrees of wickedness.**
   Matthew 12:45: The evil spirit returns with seven other spirits more wicked than Himself.

5. **Demons have faith.**
   James 2:19: "The demons also believe and tremble!"

6. **Demons like to influence people to lie.**
   Acts 5:3: Peter said to Ananias "Why has Satan filled your heart to lie to the Holy Ghost?"

7. **Demons influence people to become traitors and betray.**
   John 13:2: The devil entered Judas Iscariot to betray Jesus.

How do demons fasten on human beings? They seek out those whose makeup and temperament is most compatible to themselves, and then seek to fasten themselves onto some part of the body, or brain, or some appetite, or some faculty of the mind. When they gain access, they bury themselves into the personality of that person. If the ministry of Jesus Christ is followed as directed, it will slowly but surely force the old nature out.

Expelling of Demons

In deliverance circles the subject comes up as to how demons are expelled. We ask "What does the Bible say about it?" In pursuing this question we find that the Strong's concordance makes it very plain that a spirit is a breath. Where do we find that in scripture?

Demon Spirit: Matthew 12:43: When an "unclean spirit" (4151) is gone out of a man.

Spirit of God: Luke 4:18 Jesus: The "Spirit (4151) of the Lord is upon me.

Strong's Concordance (Greek):
Unclean spirit...4151 "Pneuma" (Greek) for breath
Spirit of God ...4151 "Pneuma" (Greek) for breath.

The Holy Spirit is associated with breath also. After His resurrection, Jesus appeared to His disciples and He breathed on them and said to them. "Receive ye the Holy Ghost". (Pneuma) (John 20:22).

Old Testament Strong's Concordance (Hebrew):
Spirits...7307...Ruwach (roo'ach) (breath).
Breath...7307...Ruwach (roo'ach) (spirit).

Genesis 2:7: God breathed into Adam's nostrils the Spirit (7307) of God and he became a living soul.

Angels
Psalm 104:4: Who maketh His angels Spirits (7307)
Hebrews 1:14: Are they not ministering Spirits (4151)

When evil spirits depart, normally they manifest through the air passages. Manifestations will be coughing, yawning, burping, a scream, belching etc. Sometimes there will be no manifestations.

Joel 2:32: Whosoever shall call on the name of the Lord shall be delivered.

Syrophenician Woman's Daughter

Matthew 15:22…The syrophenician woman said to Jesus: "My child is at home vexed with a demon!"

How did she know? A good indication of demonic activity in a person:

1. Indifference to spiritual things: Bible reading and prayer.
2. Chronic doubts or difficulty in exercising faith.
3. Unscriptural religious beliefs and practices.
4. Hatred of the blood atonement.
5. Blasphemous thoughts against God.
6. Abnormal talkativeness or loudness.
7. Muttering to oneself.
8. Shunning others.
9. Unkempt appearance.
10. Delusions.
11. Uncontrollable passions.
12. Sexual perversions.
13. Enslavement to drugs, alcohol, tobacco etc…
14. Compulsive eating.
15. Uncontrollable temper tantrums, hate etc…
16. Chronic fear anxieties.
17. Nervousness or neurotic.
18. Feelings of inadequacy or self – pity.
19. Abnormal desires for attention.
20. Abnormal bright or glazed eyes.
21. Perverse or defiant expressions.
22. Indifference.
23. Unpredictable behavior.
24. Irresponsibility.
25. Prolonged depression or gloominess.
26. Strife or discord in the Church.
27. Serious marital or parental problems.
28. Chronic physical ailments that do not respond to prayer or treatment.

Note! The Syrophenian woman being a Samaritan (not an Israelite) was an outcast. Jesus' reply to her request of her daughter's deliverance was: "Deliverance is the children's bread." But, because she recognized Jesus as her redeemer calling Him "Lord" her daughter was healed. Matthew 15:28…Jesus said to her "O'woman great is your faith!"

Deliverance
Old and New Testaments

In the Bible we (Christians) are instructed to observe the Israelite nation, how God protected them, guided them etc. We want to take a look now at how God instructed them to recapture the Promised Land. They were to capture it "Little by Little" driving the enemy out of the land. (Exodus 23:27-30) They were to completely blot out entire villages, even the livestock.

The Promised Land represents the body and the soul. The Israelites were God's chosen people and we too are God' people (by spiritual birth) but just as the Israelites had to capture the land, we too need to capture the area of our soul and body. God is in the ministry of restoration and deliverance is the way He chose to do it. (Matthew 12:28) He will keep His promise. "Ye shall know the truth and the truth shall make you free."

Notice! God told the Israelites I will drive the enemy out from the land. They occupied the land and had to be driven out. Likewise the demonic entities are in the body and soul and need to be driven out also.

Mark 16:17: And these signs shall follow them that believe. In my name shall they cast out devils: They shall speak with new tongues, they shall lay hands on the sick and they shall recover, etc.

Joshua led the Israelites into the Promised Land.
Joshua: The Hebrew form of Jesus means "Jehovah is salvation".

Deuteronomy 7:1 The Lord thy God shall bring you into the land for you. You will cast out many nations. The Hitites, the Hivites, the Canaanites, the Girgashites, Amorites and Jebusistes.

Deuteronomy 7:2 The Lord Thy God shall deliver them before thee and you shall smite them and destroy them. Show them no mercy-make no marriages with them, you shall break down their altars, break down their images, take no prisoners!

HITITES: Strong's concordance 2865-2845(Fearful one-terrorized-discourage).

CANAANITES: Strong's 3669(Humiliated-downtrodden-shame-vanquish).

JEBUSITES: Strong's 2983-947 (To tread underfoot-downtrodden-be polluted).

Judges 3:1, 2: These are the nations which the Lord left to prove Israel (vs. 2 to teach them war). Philippians 2:12b: "Work out your "salvation" with fear and trembling." Salvation "soteria" Thayer's lexicon gives the primary meaning as "Deliverance from the molestation of enemies" (work it out until you are freed).

Transfer of Spirits

Hosea 4:6 My people are destroyed for lack of knowledge.

It is important that every Christian have some knowledge of what happens in the spiritual realm when man disobeys God's laws. The Bible is a book of consequences; you obey or suffer the consequences. Satan is a legal expert, you give him legal grounds and he will take advantage of it. The transfer of spirits can take place in many ways. Let's take a look to see how that's possible.

Inheritance line: All human beings are affected by their inheritance line. (Numbers 14:18 - 3rd & 4th generations).

1. **Sin:** Cain when he sinned. (Genesis 4:11 God: Thou are cursed).

2. **Eyes:** If we yield our eyes to pornography, etc... Psalm 101:3: I will set no wicked things before my eyes.

3. **Ears:** Mark 4:24 Take heed what you hear. Rock music, Gossip-- Criticism. What should we listen to? Philippians 4:8 "Fix your thoughts on what is true and honorable and right. Think about things that are pure and lovely and admirable. Think about things that are excellent and worthy of praise."

4. **Words:** Proverbs 18:21 "Life and death are in the power of the tongue." Our tongue is a little member that we can bless and release life or curse and release death.

5. **Hands:** Our hands play an important part in the well-being of man. Mark 16:18 "They shall lay hands on the sick." I Timothy 5:22 "Lay hands suddenly on no man."

6. **Sexual sins:** I Corinthians 6:18 "Flee fornication." When a person sins through fornication, the door is open for the entrance of evil spirits.

7. **Trauma or tragedy:** The devil is no gentleman; he will take advantage of misfortune. Death of a loved one, an accident, a divorce etc. A close walk with the Lord will help the Christian and be spared.

8. **Consumption of alcohol, drugs etc:** If a person continues to drink alcohol, through alcohol spirits he can become an alcoholic, the same with drugs.

9. **Cursed objects in the home:** If you have ungodly objects in your home such as statues of Buddha, occult jewelry, symbols of witch-craft etc. (Deuteronomy 7:25).

10. **Blood transfusions:** People may contact certain viruses through blood transfusions. (HIV Etc).

Rejection

Jesus Christ Himself felt rejected when He cried out at the cross "My God, My God, why hast though forsaken me!"

Reasons for rejection:

1. **Unwanted conception:** An unclean spirit finds grounds to enter when the parents reject the child's conception.

    (A) Conceived in lust, an unwanted pregnancy results. **Note!** John the Baptist was filled with the spirit while in the womb. (A baby in the womb is capable of sensing both positive and negative spiritual influences.)

2. **Conceived too soon after marriage:**

    (A) The newly weds planned on waiting before they started their family.

3. **Conceived too close to the birth of the previous child.**

    (A) Didn't want another child so soon.

4. **Fears**:

    (A) A financial strain on the family is created.
    (B) Mother-to-be fears pain at childbirth.

5. **Conflict between parents:**

    Maybe the marriage was on the brink of divorce. It's no time to have a baby. All this has an effect on the baby.

6. **Wrong sex preference:**

    Wanted a boy, and they got a girl, wanted a girl, got a boy.

7. **Physical problems:**

    The baby was born disfigured.

8. **Divorce**:

    Is very disruptive to a young child.

9. **Verbal abuse:**
> I wish you were never born! You are stupid; you'll never amount to anything!

10. **Physical abuse:**
> As a child can take its toll.

11. **Sexual abuse:**
> One out of every four females—victim of sexual abuse. One out of every eight males-victim of sexual abuse.
> a. Fondling
> b. Sodomy
> c. Incest
> d. Rape

Note! In Sweden, incest is legal. Most prostitutes have been found to be victims of sexual abuse! More and more we are discovering how rejection can set in, even from the womb and early childhood.

Satan's Kingdom

Ephesians 6:12 "For we wrestle not against flesh and blood but against principalities, powers and rulers of darkness of this present world, against spiritual wickedness in high places."

1. **Heavenly Places (Eph. 6:12, 3:10):**
   Heavenly places are the battle ground of our spiritual warfare. Within this realm, good and evil spirits clash in the battle for men's souls.

2. **Principality (Eph. 6:12, 3:10):**
   Principalities rule over powers as well as other demonic forces. Principalities influence countries, states, cities and even Churches. They issue assignments and direct local warfare against the Church. They are the administrators of evil throughout a given area.

3. **Powers (Eph. 6:12, 3:10):**
   A power is a major demonic spirit whose primary activity is to blanket a given area with the energy of its particular evil.

4. **World rulers of darkness (Eph. 6:13):**
   A spiritual entity-on a national scale governs principalities and powers under them.

Note! In spiritual warfare it is important to remember that even though Satan is not omnipresent he has an army of unified demonic powers that have a hold on individuals, families, cities etc.

It is also equally important to learn the word of God, to be able to bind the forces of darkness that are raising havoc in society, yes, even in the Churches. Make it a point to enlist in a spiritual warfare program.

Luke 10:19: Behold, I give you power to tread upon serpents and scorpions, and over all the power of the enemy: and nothing shall by any means hurt you.

Man = A Triune being

Not until we understand the make-up of man, can we understand the real purpose of the coming of the Lord Jesus Christ. He did not come for the sole purpose to take man to heaven, but to restore that which was lost! When Adam sinned, intimacy was lost and separation came. Jesus came to redeem each one of us.

Man is made up of three parts, spirit soul and body.
Spirit: Worship-intellect-conscience
Soul: Mind-will-emotions
Body: Bone-flesh-blood

When a person comes to Christ their spirit (which was dead) is activated. It is the first phase in the Lord's plan of redemption.

1. Ephesians 2:1: You hath he quickened who were dead in trespasses and sins. (Note) you were "not" dead in your soul or body.
2. Romans 8:10: If Christ be in you the body is dead because of sin, but the "spirit is life" because of righteousness.
3. Ephesians 2:22: You who he joined together for a habitation "of the spirit."

The second phase comes as Jesus puts His discipleship program in operation. "The healing of the soul" (Body healing follows).

4. III John 2: Beloved I wish above all things that thou would prosper and be in health as thy soul prospers.
5. Romans 12:2: We are transformed by the renewing of the mind. (soul)
6. Hebrews 7:25: You are saved (sozo) to the uttermost. Saved = "sozo" (Strong's 4982) to deliver, make whole. Uttermost = (Strong's 3838) entire-whole.

This process can be accomplished only as the child of God works with God in changing our carnal nature to the divine nature. (II Peter 1:4). For instance: Luke 9:23, 24: Jesus stated "anyone who does not pick up his cross and follow me cannot be my disciple." (Luke 14:27) Why is this so important? Because it talks about losing your life. Ephesians 4:20-25: We are to put off the old nature and put on the new. (Colossians 3:8-17 also) Make it a daily practice and put on the armour of God.

Closing thoughts: A lot of Christians, even though they love the Lord are still bound up in many ways (in the soul) whether it be temper, fears, depression, lusts, pride, addictions, etc...

John 8:31, 32: If you continue in my word, then you are my disciples indeed, and ye shall know the truth and the truth shall set you free. (Truth is the legacy of Jesus Christ) we are to follow!

1 Forgiveness Prayer:

Lord, others have trespassed against me, but in obedience to Your command I now forgive each person who has ever hurt me in any way. As an act of my will I now forgive (name the person, both living and dead). Lord, bless each of these; I love them with Your love, and I ask You to forgive them also. And since You have forgiven me, I also forgive and accept myself in the name of Jesus Christ.

2 Breaking curses confession:

In the name of Jesus Christ I confess all the sins of my forefathers, and by the redemptive blood of Jesus, I now break the power of every curse passed down to me through my ancestral line. I confess and repent of each and every sin that I have committed, known or unknown, and accept Christ's forgiveness. He has redeemed me from the curse of the law. I choose the blessing and reject the curse. In the name of my Lord Jesus Christ, I break the power of every evil curse spoken against me. I cancel the force of every prediction spoken about me, whether intentionally or carelessly, that was not according to God' promised blessings. I bless those who have cursed me. I forgive each person who has ever wronged me or spoken evil of me. In the name of Jesus, I command every evil spirit of curse to leave me now. Amen!

3 Come to Jesus the Deliverer Prayer:

I come to you, Jesus, as my Deliverer. You know all my problems – the things that bind me, that torment me, that defile and harass me. I now loose myself from every dark spirit, from every evil influence, from every satanic bondage, from every spirit in me that is not the Spirit of God, and I command all such spirits to leave me now, in the name of Jesus Christ. I now confess that my body is a temple of the Holy Spirit, redeemed, cleansed and sanctified by the blood of Jesus. Therefore, Satan has no place in me, and no power over me, through the blood of Jesus.

Inheritance

Hebrews 9:15-17: States that Jesus Christ died and left the believers an inheritance. He became the testator (one who dies) and we became "heirs". Jesus not only died to give us an inheritance but He came back to instruct us how to collect it.

In order to collect our "Full inheritance" we need to submit to His discipleship program which includes deliverance!

John 14:12 Jesus: The works that I do you shall do also.

In the Old Testament Joshua was given the task to "cast out" the nations out of the "Promised Land" Deuteronomy 7:1 He was to take the land little by little Deuteronomy 7:22.

We too are to experience deliverance little by little all in God's divine time. Deliverance is a process. **Note!** Both the names of Joshua and Jesus mean "Salvation" Joshua = Old Testament, Jesus = New Testament.

When I think of inheritance I think of I John 5:14. This is the confidence that we can have in Him, that, if we "ask" anything according to His will, He hears us. That word "ask" in Strong's concordance the number is 4441. It means "A legal demand" because of the atonement it is ours. It's like we can write out a check for there is money in the bank. We don't need to beg for it. Praise God!

We need to understand that there are many reasons why a person doesn't get healed. There are legal rights of the enemy that needs to be dealt with. Un-forgiveness, curses and soul-ties need to be broke. Confess the hidden bitterness.

Inheritance

Hebrews 9:15-17 States that Jesus died and left the believers an inheritance. In order to collect a "Full inheritance" they must follow the course the Lord has instructed them to pursue. A believer must become a disciple (a soldier) and follow the legacy Jesus laid out.

John 14:12 (Jesus) The works that I do, ye shall do also.

1. Receive Jesus Christ as personal savior.

2. Water baptism.

3. Receive the baptism in the Holy Ghost.

4. Love affair with the Lord.

5. Endure suffering.

6. Forgive.

7. Love your enemies.

8. Have a systematic prayer life.

9. Learn the value of praise.

10. Enter spiritual warfare!
 A.) Realize your enemy is out to destroy your testimony!
 B.) You need to learn how to fight the fight of faith.
 C.) Be determined to take back the lost ground.
 D.) Learn how to bind and loose and take authority.
 E.) Learn to break curses. (Evil soul-ties)
 F.) Above all-count the cost.
 G.) Seek the Kingdom of God!

Len Ward's testimony of deliverance from diabetes
WWJC Jan 31st 2005

How long have you had Diabetes:
Quite a few years, it has affected other members of my family, my son, my two brothers, and my Grandmother. (She had to have her foot amputated and she went blind from Diabetes.) I took 2-pills a day.

How long have you been off your pills?
About 7 months.

How did this happen?
I attended Pastor David Middleton's Deliverance seminar in Duluth about 2 years ago. I purchased a cassette tape entitled: "Casting out demons of Diabetes" and I played it every day over a period of time. And my Blood Sugar readings have leveled off even though I'm not taking the pills. I went for my annual physical and my blood sugar was good!

Are you calling Diabetes a demon spirit!
Yes I am.

Would you explain that?
Man is a Triune being with a Spirit, Soul, and Body
Spirit – Intuition, worship, conscience.
Soul – mind, will, emotions.
Body – Flesh, bones, blood.

Ephesians 2:1: States we were dead in trespasses and sins, we weren't dead in our soul or body we were dead in our spirit!

Ephesians 2:22: States "We have a habitation with God in the spirit!"

Romans 8:16: "The Spirit itself beareth witness with our spirit, that we are the children of God."

Note! When a person gets saved, their spirit is activated, but the soul and the body are fragmented and need to be healed. That is the purpose of the discipleship program of Jesus Christ!

III John 2: Beloved, I wish above all things that you may prosper and be in good health, even as they soul prospers. When the soul starts to heal thru the Word of God, then the body follows suit.

How does Diabetes get started in a person's life?

There was no doubt in my mind that my family was under a curse of Diabetes. The Bible mentions that curses go back 3rd – 4th generations. I broke that curse of Diabetes! I confessed my sins, my family's sins and my ancestor's sins and renounced them. I took away the legal rights of the enemy and cast him out!

How do you know when a demon spirit leaves the body?

There will be a manifestation of a yawn, a cough, a burp, a belch, or a sigh generally thru the air passages. It also happens with no manifestations! Breath and spirit are the same in the word of God, "Pueuma" in the New Testament. "Ruwach" in the Old Testament. As we look at the Old Testament we see that Joshua was instructed by God to take the Promised Land little by little. To cast out the nations, the Hitites, Hivites Canaanites, Girgashites, Persites, etc. Our body is our Promised Land. Joshua = Old Testament (Nations) Jesus = New Testament (depraved nature) both mean Salvation.

The discipleship program of Jesus Christ is geared to change our nature. To drive out the depraved nature. His first sermon Luke 4:18: He stated he came to preach Deliverance to the captives! Captive = Prisoner of war (Strong's Concordance 164). Mary Magdalene – Last to see Jesus at the crucifixion – first to see Jesus after His resurrection – first to proclaim the full Gospel to disciples and the world. 7 devils were cast out of her. Mary was a woman – representing a "bride." The Church is the bride of Christ!

Chapter Two

Discipleship

We forget that Jesus was present when Adam sinned and what damage it did. In order to win a war you need an army. That's exactly what Jesus started, to mobilize when He formed the 12 disciples. A disciple is a learner (Strong's concordance). He trained those men to fight the good fight of faith using non carnal weapons. Proof in the pudding! Act 4:13 When they saw Peter and John, those unlearned and ignorant fishermen they marveled at their boldness and reminded then that they had been with Jesus.

Every Church should have an ongoing discipleship program where the parishioners could learn to fight the good fight of faith. Many families are suffering from lack of knowledge, they need to learn to bind and loose!

When Jesus left the face of this earth he said to his disciples go and make disciples. Teaching them what I have taught you. Matt. 28 (The Great Commission) Matt. 10:1 He gave the power (Dunamis) and authority to do two things 1.) Cast out demons 2.) Heal the sick.

Important references for Discipling

Why Discipleship?

GOD'S CALLING

Let us run with patience the race that is set before us.

"Looking to Jesus" the author and finisher of our faith.

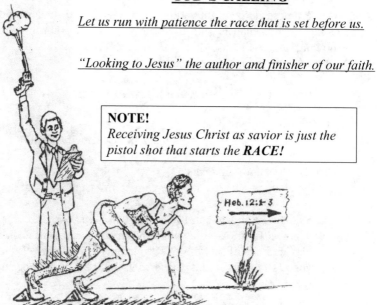

> **NOTE!**
> *Receiving Jesus Christ as savior is just the pistol shot that starts the **RACE!***

Heb. 12:1-3

If you preach to 100,000 per day with a 4% response 4,000 per day (saved-converted) 1,460,000 per year, 23,360,000 16 years.

Discipleship:
If you disciple one person for 6 months.
> Then 2 disciple 2 for 6 months.
> Then 4 disciple 4 for 6 months.
> Then 8 disciple 8 for 6 months.

At the end of 16 years: 4 Billion people 4,000,000,000

Acts 6:7 The number of disciples multiplied.
Acts 12:24 The word of God grew and multiplied

Warfare Strategies

The Christian soldier will not be quite as effective in spiritual warfare unless he has motivation. He needs first to understand that he has an enemy that is out to destroy him and ruin his testimony. Knowing this will spur him on to learn new tactics the Lord has provided, to help him win this battle.

Here are a few of them

1. Use the name of Jesus
John 14:13: Whatsoever you ask in my name I will do.

2. Use the Blood of Jesus
Revelations 12:11: They overcame him by the blood of the Lamb.

3. Ask the Father to send His angels to help you.
Hebrews 1:14: Are they not ministering spirits, sent forth for those who are heirs of salvation? Revelations 22: 8, 9 Angels are our co-workers-fellow servants. Psalms 91:10, 11 God assigns angels over our homes.

4. Pay your Tithes
Mal. 3: 8-10 God will rebuke the devourer for you

5. Use the weapon of Praise
Psalm 149: 6-7 High praises of God, to execute vengeance on the enemy.

6. Ask the Father to put a hedge around person or house.
Job 1:10God had a hedge around Job's house and family. **NOTE!** God is no respecter of persons, what He did for Job He can do for you.

7. Seek the Kingdom of God to obtain righteousness
Romans 14:17 Seek ye first the kingdom of God and His righteousness.

8. Weapon of Righteousness
   A. Isa. 54:17: No weapon formed against you shall prosper because of your righteousness.
   B. Proverbs 28:1 : The righteous are as bold as a lion
   C. Psalms 5:12: The Lord will bless the righteous and be a shield for them
   D. Psalm 5:8 Lead me O' Lord in Thy Righteousness because of my enemies.

9. Learn to bind and loose
Matthew 18:18 What ever you bind on earth is bound in heaven. What ever you loose on earth is loosed in heaven.

10. Learn to break curses
Numbers 14:18 Curses go back three and four generations, even ten. Galatians 3:13: Christ redeemed man from the curse of the law. Other curses weren't eliminated, he's given man the power to break the curses.

11. Put on your armor every day
Ephesians 6:11: God has provided protection—use it!

12. Pick up your cross every day
Luke 9:23-24 What does picking up your cross mean? It simply means that you are going to work with God to die to self, die to the old nature. You are to do it daily. To put off the old and put on the new.

1. **Put off** selfishness, greediness—**Put on** agape love.
2. **Put off** fear—**Put on** courage and holy boldness.
3. **Put off** all lusts—**Put on** righteousness, holiness, godliness and purity.
4. **Put off** all lying, anger, wrath, blasphemy, filthy communication—**Put on** kindness, meekness, humility and longsuffering.

"Truth"

It seems that everyone is quoting (John 8:31, 32) these days. "ye shall know the truth and the truth shall set you free." It is revealed in scripture that there is only one truth, and that is Jesus Christ. (John 14:6) Jesus: "I am the way, the truth, and the life."

If Jesus Christ is the truth, then we should take heed to what he says in his instructions to the Church: Mark 16:17: These signs shall follow believers, in my name they shall cast out devils, speak with new tongues, and heal the sick. The questions comes up, if the Church is to cast out demons, out of whom? To answer this question we need to again go to the author, Jesus Christ.

John 17:9 Jesus: "Father, I pray not for the world (unbelievers) but I pray for them which thou hast given me." Note! Jesus was always bent on building up the Church. To shed the carnal nature, to take on the "Jesus Nature."

Jesus stated in (John 14:12) the works that I do, you shall do also. Jesus cast demons out of believes and instructed the Church to do the same. Deliverance is not for unbelievers. Matthew 12:43-45: Says that the demons will come back seven times greater. Unbelievers don't want any part of it anyway. Many quote (II Corinthians 5:17) that when a person receives the Lord as personal savior they become a new creation. Therefore, how can they have any demonic problems? The Holy Spirit and a demon cannot dwell in the same body.

To receive a revelation of this we need to center our thoughts on (I Thessalonians 5:23) Man is a triune being, spirit, soul and body. When a person receives the Lord as savior the Spirit is activated. **Note!** When Adam sinned the spirit died, now it is alive. (Ephesians 2:1) we were dead in trespasses and sins, we were not dead in our soul. (Mind-will and emotions) nor our body. (Bones-flesh and the blood) we were dead in the spirit.

The word has a lot to say about the soul, how important it is. Because of sin it has become fragmented, curses and evil soul-ties have taken their toll.

It is because of the depravity of man the ministry of Jesus Christ comes into focus. His discipleship program is designed to drive out the demonic entities that have had their way too long. Many Christians, Yes, even pastors have been driven by demon spirits of lusts, fears, condemnation, temper, depression etc. This should not be! Jesus came to set people free.

Hebrews 9:15-17: Jesus died and left us an inheritance, not only that, but He came back to teach us how to acquire the "full inheritance," and restore the intimacy that Adam had with God. Romans 12:2 We are transformed by the renewing of the mind. (Soul) "God's perfect will!"

When the soul gets healthy, then the person becomes healthy. III John 2 Beloved, I wish above all things, that you prosper and be in health, even "as your soul prospers." Isn't' it strange, that Mary Magdalene was the first to see Jesus after His resurrection? Mary was a woman, the "Bride". The bride represents "The Church." Jesus cast seven demons out of Mary. (I wonder what the Lord is trying to tell us!) Isn't it strange, that both Joshua and Jesus' names mean "salvation"? Joshua was given the task of driving out the nations out of the "Promised Land." (The Hitites-Hivites-Perzities-Canaanites-Gergashites.) Jesus was given the task of driving out the old "Adamic nature".

The Making of a Disciple
Disciple = Learner

It is important that the Church of the Lord Jesus Christ receive his final instructions as he left the face of this earth. He stated "Go and make disciples." What is a disciple? A Disciple is a learner, he learns how to fight the good fight of faith, and he is a soldier. Jesus came to evangelize yes, but the thrust of His ministry was to build an army with the power of righteousness. He started with the twelve apostles, then the seventy, and now the rest of us. What is it that a disciple learns?

1. Learns to discipline his life. (Obedience)
2. Learns how to think.(The renewing of the mind)
3. Learns how to talk. (Lives/death is in the power of the tongue)
4. Learns how to love. (To have the compassion of Jesus)
5. Learns how to fight. (The Jesus way)
6. Learns how to face trials. (With courage and Holy boldness)
7. Learns to fear the Lord, (desperately needed to fight evil)
8. Learns how to worship. (Anointed worship)
9. Learns how to be like Jesus. (In all circumstances)
10. Learns how to persevere. (To be steadfast in all situations)
11. Learns how to discern. (To recognize the enemy)
12. Learns how to pray. (To take authority, to bind and loose)
13. Learns how to endure. (Important, as testing will come)

Matthew 28:18-20:
Jesus: All power is given to me on heaven and earth, go ye therefore and "make disciples," baptizing them in the name of the Father, the Son and the Holy Ghost. (Bury the old nature) teaching them the things that I have commanded you. What did Jesus command them to do? To answer that we need to go to.

Matthew 10:1:
And when He had called unto Him His twelve disciples, He gave them power to cast out devils and to heal the sick.

Luke 9:1, 2:
> Then He called His twelve disciples together, and gave them power and authority over all devils, and to cure diseases. Then He sent them out to preach the kingdom of God, and to heal the sick.

Matthew 6:33:
> Seek ye first the kingdom of God and His righteousness.

Power of Righteousness

The Goal for every Christian should be that he might be in the will of the Lord. With that comes a peace that passeth all understanding. So it's important that we find out what is God's will. As always we need to look no further than Jesus Christ. He came to make disciples; He came to make mature soldiers who would have the power of righteousness.

1. I Samuel 18:12: Even though King Saul had all power, he feared David because the Lord was with him.
2. Psalm 105:38 The Israelites were slaves to the Egyptians, yet the Egyptians feared them.
3. Exodus 12: 35, 36: The Egyptians also lent to the Israelites all the things they required.
4. Mark 6:20: King Herod feared John because he knew he was a just and holy man.
5. John 7:44: Jesus passed thru the midst of them. (Many a time people wanted to kill Jesus but couldn't because of His righteousness.) (see Luke 4:28-30)
6. Acts 6:10 (Stephen) They were not able to resist the wisdom and the spirit by which he spoke.
7. Joshua 4:14 The people feared Joshua as they did Moses.
8. Joshua 9:24 The inhabitants of the land were sore afraid of God's people.
9. Proverbs 29:27 he that is upright is an abomination to the wicked.

Power of the Tongue

There was good reason why the Lord Jesus said what He did in the Great Commission. He stated "Go ye therefore and make disciples." A disciple is a learner; he learns how to discipline his life. One of the most important is that he learns what to say and just as important, learns what not to say. We have an enemy (Satan) waiting for a chance to gain legal rights because of a negative statement that we make.

Proverbs 18:21 "Life and death are in the power of the tongue and those who love it will eat its fruits."

James 3:3-12 The tongue is a small thing but what damage it can do.

1. A great forest can be set on fire by one tiny spark!
2. A tiny rudder can turn a huge ship!
3. A small bit can make a large horse turn around!

What we say is not emphasized enough in the Christian realms. It's important! What we speak or confess either builds or destroys our faith.

Some of the quotes many Christians make:
1. "I don't have any faith!"
2. "I just know I'll need an operation!"
3. "I always get the flu this time of the year!"
4. "I could never get up early to pray!"

Numbers 13:30 "Of the twelve spies that went into the Promised Land, only Joshua and Caleb said "We are able!" The other ten said "We are not able!" (They paid the consequences). Think before you speak!

Early Rising

Many of God's servants in the Bible had the habit of rising early. Many have found out that it is the key to the intimacy of God. As we read the Old Testament we see that the Israelites had to gather the manna "before the sun had risen."

Note! It is important to seek the Lord early, to give Him the first fruits of your day. It gets you on His wave length, to be led by the spirit the rest of the day.

Examples of rising early

1. Abraham...Rose up early. (Genesis 19:27, 21:14, 22:3).
2. Jacob...Rose up early. (Genesis 28:18)
3. Moses...Rose up early. (Exodus 8:20, 9:13, 24:4, 34:4)
4. Joshua...Rose up early. (Joshua 3:1, 6:12, 7:16, 8:10)
5. Gideon...Rose up early. (Judges 6:38)
6. Hannah...Rose up early. (I Samuel 1:19)
7. Samuel...Rose up early. (I Samuel 15:12)
8. David...Rose up early. (I Samuel 17:20)
9. Job...Rose up early. (Job 1:5)
10. The apostles...Entered the temple at daybreak. (Acts 5:21)
11. The Lord Jesus (Mark 1:35)

The word disciple comes from the word discipline. The disciple is a learner, he learns how to conduct his life as a soldier. A soldier at first does not comprehend what war is all about, he then receives teaching on how the enemy is operates, he hears of the atrocities, the sneak attacks of the enemy. He hears how his fellow soldiers were gunned down in a ruthless way. All of a sudden it finally downs on him what is taking place and his attitude changes. He's determined to do what ever he can to promote his superior's program. "He becomes war minded."

It is the same in the Christian realm, until the Christian soldier learns how Satan has made a mess out of peoples live, it doesn't phase him too much at first. After a while it finally sinks in that Satan is the root of the problem and its pay back time. He realizes that his calling is to see people set free. He acquires a new mindset. He becomes spiritual warfare minded!

Note! There are two reasons that will get you out of bed for prayer early in the morning.

1. Your love for the lord and
2. Your hatred for the devil.
   Psalm 97:10 Ye that love the Lord, "Hate evil."

Jesus: Our example

Philippians 2:7 Jesus made himself of no reputation and took upon himself the form of a servant. Reputation (to make empty). Emptied himself of all the benefits of being God to become like man.

John 14:12 The works that I do ye shall do also.
John 17:18 As the Father sent me, so send I you.
John 20:21 As the Father sent me, so send I you.
Revelations 3:21 As I overcometh, you too will overcome.

Matthew 11:29 (Jesus) Take my yoke upon you, and learn of me!

Note! Jesus always set a precedent for His disciples to follow. For instance, His "water baptism," by John. Water baptism is symbolic of burying the old nature. Jesus didn't' need to be baptized because he didn't have the "old nature." He wanted to set an example. He was also filled with "Dunamis power" at the same time. Why? Because he had emptied himself and now was preparing himself for ministry. (Luke 4:1, 14)

We too need to follow Jesus in preparing for our ministry! He is the truth that will set you and others free! Jesus was sinless...but we have (I John 1:9) Jesus didn't' have curses to deal with...but we have? (Galatians 3:13) Our goal: To have the power of righteousness, like Jesus!

Healing the Fragmented soul

The importance of the soul

1. Deut. 4:29 "We seek the Lord with our soul."
2. Deut. 6:5 "We love the Lord with our soul."
3. Deut. 10:12 "We serve the Lord with our soul."
4. Deut 11:18 "We store God's word with our soul."
5. Deut. 30:10 "We obey God's word with our soul."
6. Psalm 142:7 "We praise the Lord with our soul."

How does the soul become fragmented?

1. Prov. 15:32 "By refusing instruction.
2. Prov. 6:32 "Committing adultery. (Destroys one's soul).
3. Psalm 106:15 "Disobedience. (I'll do it my way) (God sent leanness into their soul)
4. Psalm 22:24 "Make no friendship with an angry man. (You'll receive a snare in your soul).
5. Psalm 41:4 "Sinning against the Lord. (Prov. 8:36) (Ii peter 2:7 "Lot's soul was vexed by environment).

How to get your soul healthy

1. I Peter 1:22 "Purify the soul by obeying the truth.
2. Prov. 16:17 "Departing from evil, preserves the soul.
3. Prov. 16:24 "Choose good company, bad vexes the soul.
4. James 1:21 "Receive words with meekness-save the soul.

III John 2 "Beloved, I wish above all things that you would prosper and be in health, even as thy soul prospereth.

    A. Psalm 43:22 "The Lord redeemeth the soul of His servants.
    B. Psalm 72:14 "He shall redeem my soul
    C. Psalm 69:18 "Draw nigh unto my soul and redeem it! (Deliver me because of my enemies)
    D. Psalm 49:15 "But God will redeem my soul from the power of the grave.

Redeem = To buy back –to repurchase- to liberate form captivity or bondage to deliver- to rescue.

Romans 12:2 "We are transformed by the renewing of our minds.

Defensive vs. Offensive

There is a trend in the Christian circles that a Christian is to take a defensive stand in our dealings with the devil. They quote Eph. 6:13 "And above all, stand." Joshua would have never taken the "Promised Land" if all he did was to stand!

We too will never take our "Promised Land" our spirit – soul and body. We need to take the offensive!! And hit the devil hard!

Chapter Three

Kingdom of God

As we are nearing the end of the age, many things are happening that reveal to us that Satan is coming in like a flood. The question arises, what will the Christians' standard be to combat this aggression? To answer that we need to take a good look at the spiritual giants and see how they overcome, starting with the Lord Jesus Christ.

1. **Jesus = (Luke 4:43) Jesus state:** I must preach "The Kingdom of God" to other cities also. Luke 4:33 "Jesus had delivered a man of an unclean spirit in the synagogue. Luke 4:40 "many were healed and delivered!

2. **Paul (Acts 20:27) Paul stated:** For I have not shunned to declare unto you the "full counsel of God" (Acts 20:25) The preaching of "The kingdom of God" is declaring the full counsel of God! (Acts 28:31) Paul preached the Kingdom of God. (teaching things that concern the Lord Jesus Christ)

3. **Philip (Acts 8:12) Philip preached "The kingdom of God?** (Acts 8:5-7_ for unclean spirits came out of many crying with a loud voice!

4. **Jesus (Mark 1:14, 15) Jesus preached "The kingdom of God." He stated:** The time is fulfilled; the "Kingdom of God" is at hand! Repent ye and believe the gospel. (The good news) Mark 1:21, 22 "They were astonished at His doctrine! Mark 1:23 "Deliverance was done in Church with Jesus casting out unclean spirits. I Cor. 15:24 "Then cometh the end, when He (Jesus) shall have delivered up the Kingdom to God, even the Father, when He shall have put down all rule and all authority and power. (Dunamis)

Important references for the Kingdom of God

What is the "Kingdom of God?

I Cor. 4:20 "The Kingdom of God is not in word, but in power. (The power of God in the flesh).

Matt. 12:28 "But if I cast out devils by the spirit of God, then The Kingdom of God has come upon you.

Heb. 1:2 "Hath in these last days, God has spoken unto us by His son Jesus!

Note! The time has come to listen to the voice of Jesus. Jesus is truth; it's the truth that will set you free!

God's plan of restoration
"Preaching the Kingdom of God"

Matt. 6:33 "Seek ye first the Kingdom of God and His righteousness!"

1. Mark 1:14, 15 & Luke 4:43 "Jesus preached the Kingdom of God.
2. Luke 9:1, 2 "Jesus gave the disciples power and authority, then sent them out to preach the kingdom of God.
3. Luke 9:60 "Jesus sends the disciples out to preach the Kingdom of God.
4. Luke 9:27 (Jesus) "But I tell you of a truth, there be some standing here, which shall not taste of death, till they see the kingdom of God."
5. Mark 16:17 "Jesus now sends "us" out to preach the Kingdom of God.
    A. Cast out devils
    B. Heal the sick
    C. Speak with new tongues

Chapter Four

Prayer

Jesus' Prayer Life

As we survey the prayer of our Lord's earthly life, it becomes obvious that prayer was the foundation upon which our Lord built a life of perfect obedience.

1. **Our Lord prayed when unpopular**
   Luke 6:11 "The scribes and Pharisees were filled with madness."
   Luke 6:12 "Jesus went out to the mountain and prayed all night."

2. **Our Lord prayed when suffering**
   Luke 22:44 "In the Garden of Gethsemane he prayed more earnestly: and His sweat were as great drops of blood falling down.

3. **Our Lord opened and closed His ministry with prayer**.
   Luke 3:21 "Jesus being baptized and praying.
   Luke 23:24 (Jesus) "Father forgive them" as he hung on the cross!

4. **Our Lord prayed when joyful.**
   Luke 10:17 "When the 70 returned announcing victory over the enemy, Jesus rejoiced in His spirit saying "I thank thee heavenly Father!"

5. **Prayer had priority over His social life.**
   Matt. 14:23 "Our Lord sent the multitude away and went up into the mountain to pray.

6. **Prayer had priority over His physical rest.**

Luke 6:12 "Before He chose the disciples He went up the mountain and continued all night in prayer.

7. Our Lord prayed "Early in the Morning!"
Mark 1:35 "And in the morning, rising up a great while before day, He went out, and departed into a solitary place, and there He prayed."

Important references for Prayer

Prayer I

1. What is prayer? Simply defined: Prayer is enjoying fellowship with God. It can develop sensitivity between our spirit and His spirit.

2. Three reasons for prayer.
    A. Prayer created fellowship: Jesus frequently got alone with the Father. (Matt. 14:23).
    B. Prayer renews us spiritually: It refreshes the presence and glory of God.
    C. Prayer makes us co-laborers with God: Through prayer we share the burdens and concerns of God.

3. Jesus Christ is our example and teacher.
By watching the miracles and life of Jesus, the disciples could see the connection of divine power and prayer.

4. Praying with faith:
Mark 11:22, 24 "Whatever things you ask for when you pray, believe that you will receive and you will have them.

5. Praying in the Holy Ghost:
Jude 20 "But ye beloved, building yourselves up on your most holy faith, praying in the Holy Ghost. (Tongues)

6. Praise and thanksgiving:
Psalm 100:4 "Begin with praise and thanksgiving."
Psalm 22:3 "God inhabits the praises of His people."

7. Make petitions and supplications:
Phil. 4:6 "Let your requests known unto God."

8. Personal examination:
Psalm 51:10 "Create in me a clean heart O' God, and renew a right spirit within me.

9. Praying in the name of Jesus:

Co. 3:17 "Whatever you do in thought, word and deed, do all in the name of Jesus.

Note! You do not pray to Jesus-you pray to the Father in the name of Jesus.

10. Want your prayers answered?

John 9:31 "Be a worshipper and seek the Lord's will, plan to be alone with Him early each day.

Prayer II

Set a definite time for prayer. Here are some suggestions to help in prayer. First of all make sure you have forgiven everyone! Enter your prayer time with praise and thanksgiving! Psalm 22:3 "God inhabits the praises of His people."

1. **Seek God early.**
   A. Gen. 19:27 "Abraham prayed "early" for Sodom."
   B. Ex. 24:4 "Moses went up to the mountain "early"."
   C. I Sam. 1:19 "Hannah prayed "early"."
   D. Psalm 143:8 David prayed "early"
   E. Mark 1:35 Jesus prayed "early"

2. **How to pray**
   A. Make a list, then be led to pray for others.
   B. Fall asleep? Start walking and praying.
   C. Pray with pen and paper in hand.
   D. Pray in heavenly language.

3. **Put on the armour!**
   A. Rom. 13:14 "Put ye on the Lord Jesus Christ!"

4. **Pray with persistence.** (Don't give up!)

5. **Learn to bind and loose.** (Matt. 18:18) (Matt. 12:29

6. **Learn to break curses –evil soul-ties.**

7. **Learn to put a hedge around your loved ones.** (Job 1:10) (Hosea 2:6).

8. **Learn to resist and rebuke the enemy.** (James 4:7), (Matt.17:18) (Mark 9:25)

Last but not least, be sure to praise all thru the day! Psalm 71:8 "Let my mouth be filled with thy praise and with thy honor "all the day."

Prayer III

Before setting out to effectively pray and get results we must prepare ourselves. Make sure you don't have any un-forgiveness etc. There might be times when it's a situation that' difficult to pray. The following is a sample of those occasions.

1. A person who has cancer.
   Heavenly father, I bring _____ to the throne of grace and I ask for a miracle of healing for (Him/her). I cover _____ with the blood of Jesus and I curse this cancer and command it to be destroyed at its very roots, to loose its hold on_____. Thank you Father for Jesus, in His name I pray. Amen

2. A young man who is on drugs, left home. His mother doesn't know where he is. Heavenly Father, I bring _____ to the throne of grace and I ask for the power of your anointing in this prayer. Please send angels to find my son. (Heb. 1:14) I bind the strongman in him; also I bind all rebellion, stubbornness, disobedience and anti-submissiveness. I ask this in Jesus name. Amen

3. A woman who has left the witches.
   A. Ask the Father to put a hedge around her. (Hosea 2:6) Ask for angel protection. (Psalm 91:11)
   B. Break all curses that would be coming at her.
   C. Break all evil soul-ties with the witches' coven.
   D. Bind all fears, anxieties in Jesus name!

4. For unsaved loved one.
   Heavenly Father, I bring my unsaved loved ones to the throne of grace. I bind all deception, lack of conviction, apathy, lethargy, pride, self righteousness, religious spirits, anti Christ's spirits and all the work of the enemy that would hinder the promptings of the Holy Spirit. May Godly sorrow come upon them that brings on repentance. Amen.

Some suggestions: Rise early for prayer-have a set time. Be sure to read the word, even a proverb a day at least. Put on the armor piece by piece. Get in tune with the Lord; keep Him in focus throughout the day with praise and thanksgiving. It pays big dividends.

Prayer IV
Prayer for lost loved one's

Often times we grow weary of praying for lost loved one's. You ask yourself "are they ever going to find the Lord?" We must remember that God's ways are not our ways, that His word is still guidelines for our faith walk as we obey His word, we must trust him to produce the results.

I Cor. 10:11 States that the Israelites were our examples that we can learn from their doings.

Let's go to the book of Joshua. He was given the task of taking the city of Jericho. There are three things we can learn from Jericho in regards to our unsaved loved ones.

First, base everything on the promise of God.
Joshua 6:2 Lord said to Joshua: "See I have given into thine hand Jericho." Now relate that to the Lord's promise to save your loved ones. "See, I have given salvation of your family." Take the promise. (Acts 16:31)

Second Faith and not by sight.
The walls looked the same every time the Israelites went around the city of Jericho. (No cracks showed in the walls.) How easy it would be to doubt, but the promise of God is still good. Joshua and his men refused to doubt. We see no change in our loved ones, but we don't' go on what we see, we go on faith. (Acts 16:31) also (II Cor. 5:7)

Third a lesson on praising God.
Joshua 6:16 "Shout! For the Lord hath given you the city!" Remember: Joshua shouted while the walls were still standing. Are you praising the Lord for a lost loved one?

Prayer for the family

Ever since Adam sinned in the Garden of Eden, Satan has had a field day in ruling people's lives. Sin has taken its toll and the depravity of man has brought on curses, evil soul-ties etc.

Jesus Christ came to restore, to give His followers the power (Dunamis) to overcome the enemy, and return the intimacy that Adam lost. He gave His disciple the authority to bind and loose, now He's given it to us.

Luke 10:19 "I give you power to tread upon serpents and scorpions and over all the power of the enemy.

Matt. 18:18 "And whatsoever you bind and loose on earth shall be bound and loosed in heaven.

Prayer:
Lord, I bring my saved and unsaved loved ones to the throne of grace.

1. I bind deception.
2. I bind lack of conviction.
3. I bind apathy-lethargy-passivity.
4. I bind pride.
5. I bind self righteousness.
6. I bind religious spirits.
7. I bind anti-Christ spirits.
8. I bind un-forgiveness-bitterness-hatred-anger-temper.
9. I bind all addictions-alcohol-drugs etc.
10. I resist the enemy and command him to loose his hold on my family. I break all curses – third and fourth generations back the curse of poverty, continued emotional and mental confusion, sickness and pain, continued female complications, marriage breakdown, accident prone, stolen property, robbing God of tithes and offerings, abortion,

children out of wedlock, gambling, Alzheimer's, alcohol and drugs, gluttony, diabetes etc.

Numbers 14:18, Exodus 20:5, Psalm 78:8, Lamentations 5:7

Galatians 3:13 "Jesus Christ became a curse for us on the cross.

Prayer: Father, send your angels to minister to my family. Minister truth-conviction of sin-godly sorrow that worketh repentance- the spirit of adoption and the fear of the Lord. Amen.

Acts 16:31 "believe on the Lord Jesus Christ and though shall be saved, "And they house."

Prayer over the phone

As we learn spiritual warfare there will be times when people will call you for prayer over the phone. We want to be as effective as we can and this prayer can be used for the person in need of healing.

Heavenly Father I bring _____ to the throne of grace and I ask for the power of your anointing in this prayer that would heal _____.

Forgive us of any sins that would hinder the healing action that is taking place in _____ even right now.

I bind you devil and place the blood of Jesus Christ between us, you will not hinder this prayer. I wash _____ in the blood of Jesus.

Devil, we cancel your assignment and retake all the ground you have gained. I break all curses, evil soul-ties, physic sources from our ancestors, all self imposed curses, all legal rights that would hinder _____ healing.

I speak directly to this _____ and curse it, just as Jesus cursed the fig tree. I command it to be destroyed at its very roots.

I claim Galatians 3:13 to break every curse, also I peter 2:24. I claim healing for _____; by the stripes of Jesus (He/she is healed.) I pray that (His/Her) health would be restored as an eagle's. I thank you that you are our God that heals all diseases. Amen.

Gal. 3:13 Christ hath redeemed us form the curse of the law, being made a curse for us.

I Peter 2:24 who his own self bare our sins in his own body on the tree. That we being dead to sins, should live unto righteousness: By whose strips ye were healed.

Psalm 91

Following the Lord is a two-way operation and Psalm 91 reveals this in a marvelous way. It is divided into three parts and it is very encouraging to see the benefits that Lord bestows to those who choose to follow and obey Him.

You make your choice　　　　　　**Your Benefits**

1. Shall abide under protection of God. (vs.1)

2. God shall be my refuge-fortress. (vs.2)

Psalm 91:1 You choose: To dwell in a secret place.

3. I will be delivered from snare of the fowler. (vs. 3)

4. I will be delivered from noise some pestilence. (vs. 3) Noisome=unbearable

5. Covered with God's protection (feathers). (vs. 4)

6. God will be my shield and buckler. (vs. 4) (From the darts of the enemy)

7. Keep me from fear. (vs. 5)

8. God will show us the punishment of the wicked. (vs. 8)

1. No evil shall befall thee. (vs. 10)

2. Protection-even my house. (vs. 5)

3. Angels are sent out especially for you. (vs. 11)

4. They will protect unless you sin. (vs. 12) (Read Psalm 125:1-3)

5. You will trample the enemy. (vs. 13) (Read Mark 16:17, 18 and Luke 10:19)

> Psalm 91:9
> Because you have made the Lord thy habitation.

1. You will be delivered. (From your old life) (vs. 14)

2. You will be set up (not down) (vs. 14)

3. You will call and I will answer. (vs. 15)

4. In trouble-God will be with you. (vs. 15) (Deliver him-honor him)

5. You will live longer. (vs. 16)

6. God will show you your salvation. (vs. 16)

> Psalm 91:14
> Because you have chosen to love (obey) me; to know my Name.

Prayer against fear

I come to you Lord Jesus as my deliverer. You know all my problems. The things that bind me, that torment me, that defile and harass me.

I confess to you today that I've had many fears. I have not trusted you. I have sinned against you and I ask you to forgive me. I forgive everyone who has ever wronged me and I take back all legal rights of the enemy.

I now break every curse that has caused me to have fear, I renounce them in Jesus name. God has not given to me a spirit of fear, but power, love and a sound mind. You spirit of fear, I take authority over you from the power of the third heaven and I command that you leave me now. Thank you Lord for the victory that I can have in you.

I come against the:

Fear of rejection, fear of accidents, fear of death, fear of animals, fear of close places, fear of crowds, fear of demons, fear of heights, fear of failure, fear of the future, fear of dogs, fear of accusation, fear of men, fear of women, fear of condemnation, fear of lost salvation, fear of doctors, fear of responsibility, fear of the dark, fear of water, fear of reproof, fear of disapproval, fear of authority, fear of god, fear of judgment, fear of man.

I command all such spirits to leave me now in Jesus name!! Amen!
Take a deep breath and let it go.

Chapter Five

Knowledge

Hosea 4:6 My people are destroyed for lack of knowledge.

I went to the super market for my wife. I filled up the cart with items from my wife's shopping list and checked out. When I got to the car I reached in my pocket for my keys and found a bunch of coupons! She spent a lot of time cutting them out! No. I didn't tell her. Isn't it the same way for a lot of Christians who are running around with a fist full of spiritual coupons but won't cash them in to help themselves and others. (The baptism of the Holy Spirit-Deliverance-Healing).

Two Pastors took their dogs duck hinting. A duck flew over them and one of the Pastors shot it, his dog jumped into the water and retrieved it. The other pastor shot a duck also and his dog retrieved the duck walking on water" This happened a few more times. Finally the one pastor said to his friend. Didn't you see my dog walking on the water? His Pastor friend turned and said, "Can't swim, can he?"

Hosea 4:6 My people are destroyed for lack of knowledge, because they have rejected knowledge, I will reject them and their children. (As a parent your stupidity can actually cause a curse upon your children)

Through the lack of knowledge Satan gained the upper hand. He is having a field day and we need to call his hand. We need to cry out to God to give us a hunger for His knowledge and truth, His written word—the Bible.

When I was sailing on the ore boats on the great lakes years ago before I was saved! We played poker every evening. I can remember this big pot and there was only two of us left. He would raise me and I did likewise. I called him to show his cards and he had a four flush. I showed my full house and raked in the pot. Satan is a deceiver also.

God made you to glorify himself. Adam and Eve were very special to God, more so than any thing else he made. Adam and Eve were made in the image of God, beautifully and wonderfully and uniquely made. Ever person born is different from every one else. God made you in His perfect timing so that he might be glorified. God made a beautiful place for Adam and eve but through the knowledge of good and evil sin came into Adam and eve. God had to make a way to redeem mankind form this terrible sin.

You are beautifully, wonderfully and uniquely made.

The Bible is the longest and most accurate recorded history about mankind. If you base your beginning out the facts then the bible is what you want to follow.

Important references for Knowledge

Signs of the times

Luke 12:54-56 Jesus said to the people, when ye see a cloud rise out of the west, straightway ye say, "there cometh a shower," and so it is. When you see the south wind blow, ye say "There will be heat and so it is." "Ye hypocrites! Ye can discern the face of the sky and the earth but how is it that ye do not discern this time?"

1. II Tim. 3:1 This know also, that in the last days perilous times shall come.

2. I Tim. 4:1 That in the latter times some shall depart form the faith.

3. Matt. 24:7 There shall be famines, pestience's, nation shall rise against nation.

4. Matt. 24:4 Take heed! That no man deceive you!

5. Jude 1:18 Abnormal sex activity. (There will be mockers in the last time, who will walk after their own ungodly lusts).

6. The absence of gifted leadership. (In preparation for the anti-Christ)

7. II Tim. 3:2, 3 (Lawlessness will prevail) for men shall be lovers of their own selves, covetous, boasters, proud, blasphemers, disobedient to parents, unthankful, unholy, without natural affection, trucebreakers false accusers, incontinent, fierce, despisers of those that are good.

8. Dan. 12:4 An increase in speed and knowledge.

9. I Tim. 4:1-3 There will be intense demonic activity. (many will give heed to seducing spirits, and doctrines of devils).

10. Population explosion! (Almost six billion people on the earth!)

11. Rev. 9:15, 16 The Bible prophesies a 200 million man army will launch a war (today China can field a 200 million man army)

12. Rev. 16:12 The Euphrates River to be dried up. The conditions for fulfilling this 1900 year prophecy are now in place. A huge reservoir has been built by Turkey that could stop the flow of the Euphrates River for a period of time.

13. Rev. 13: The Bible prophesies a world dictator will soon rule over a world government. A world wide numbering system is now possible because of the computer.

Matt. 28:18-20 Before Jesus' departure he instructed the apostles to go and make disciples, teaching them spiritual warfare, preparing them for the end times. It is also important for the body of Christ to learn spiritual warfare in preparing for the end times. Persecution is just around the corner. ***Be Ready!!***

There are many who are serving the Lord with the desire to go on to maturity, to be able to overcome the enemy and acquire the abundant life that is promised. Well, there is only one way and that is thru God's word! Meditate on it, memorize it, and it will get you strong in the Lord. (Victories will come)

Joshua 1:8 Meditate on the word and your way will be prosperous and have good success.

Importance of the word of God

1. Jesus is the word
   John 1:14 The word became flesh and dwelt among us.

2. Healing
   Prov. 4:20 Attend unto my words, for they are life to those who find them and health to their flesh.

3. Prevention against sin
   Psalm 119:11 "They word have I hid in my heart, that I might not sin against thee.

4. Helps get your requests answered
   If my words abide in you, you shall ask and it will be given you.

5. Weapon against the enemy
   Luke 4:4 when Jesus came out of the wilderness and confronted by Satan, he answered "It is written."

6. Obtain faith
   Rom. 10:17 Faith cometh by hearing and hearing by the word of God.

7. It is the pathway to holiness
   I Peter 1:16 "Be ye holy as I am holy saith the Lord!"
   (Only one way to get holy-thru the word of God).

8. The doorway to discipleship
   John 8:31 Jesus: If you continue in my word, then you are my disciples indeed!

Spiritual warfare
Purpose of the holy word of God

1. Adam/God (Sweet fellowship) intimacy-love affair.

2. Adam sinned (Loss of fellowship-loss of intimacy)

3. Sin brought on: Curses-evil soul-ties – depravity of man-Satan became the god of this world.

4. Jesus was present when sin came into focus. He witnessed the results (John 1:2)

5. God declares war on Satan, His plan of restoration was put into motion. (Gen 3:15)

6. Joshua was given the task to occupy the Promised Land. To cast out the nations the Hitites, the Hivites, the Canaanites, Gergashites, Persites etc. (Deut. 7:1) Joshua=salvation (Strong's) (Old Testament) (Little by little)

7. Jesus came on the scene, was crucified, and took on our sins.

8. Jesus came back and put his discipleship program into motion.
   A. 12 disciples
   B. 70 disciples
   C. Present Christians. (Mark 16:17)
      Jesus = salvation (Strong's) (New Testament)

9. Purpose of His discipleship plan: To drive out the Adamic nature and to restore that which was lost. (The intimacy with God.)

10. Process of Jesus' discipleship agenda.
    Man is a triune being- spirit, soul and body. (I Thess. 5:23). (Spirit= intuition- worship-conscience) (Soul=mind-will-emotions) (Body=bones-flesh-blood). When a man comes to

the Lord, his spirit is activated. His soul and body is fragmented and demonized! (Eph. 2:1)

11. Jesus' discipleship program is designed to heal the soul and the body. (III John 2)

12. Jesus commanded the people to go to Jerusalem until the Holy Spirit comes. (Acts 1:4)

13. Upon receiving the baptism in the Holy Ghost they would have the power (Dunamis) to drive out the carnal nature. (John 14:12)

14. Through the discipleship program of Jesus Christ, deliverance from the old Adamic nature would manifest and intimacy with the Lord would return. (Little by little) Fellowship with the Lord is restored!

Jesus Christ is coming back for a Church without spot or wrinkle!

DON'T GIVE UP!

Backsliding

Usually backsliding does not manifest all at once, but will be birthed by the mind going astray. The old story of the frog boiled in water is true in every Christian. It may not seem harmless at first but Satan will take advantage of every opportunity to get his foot in the door. It is important that every child of God seek the Lord before he starts his day. To set his mind on God!

Isa. 26:3 Thou will give perfect peace, whose mind is stayed on thee.

The case of the apostle Peter

1. Matt. 26:33 He boasted. (Pride)
2. Matt. 26:33 He made Jesus a liar! Jesus said "all" (vs. 31)
3. Matt. 26:40 He slept instead of prayed.
4. Matt. 26:41 He failed to mortify the flesh.
5. Matt. 26.51 He relied on the arm of the flesh.
6. Matt. 26:56 He forsook Christ and fled.
7. Matt. 26:58 He followed "far off".
8. Matt. 26:58 He sat with the Lord's enemies.
9. Matt. 26:58 He gave up hope. (Discouraged)
10. Matt 26:68-72 He became afraid. (Fear of man)
11. Matt 26: 68-72 He lied.
12. Matt. 26: 69-72 He cursed.

Luke 22:31-34 Jesus predicted Peter's backsliding and his recovery. He prayed for Peter.

The mind is the battlefield (Guard it!) II Cr. 10:5 Casting down imaginations and every high thing that exalts itself against the knowledge of God and bringing into captivity "every" thought to the obedience of Christ. Psalm 97:10 Ye that love the Lord, hate evil! John 10:10 The enemy comes to steal, kill, and destroy.

II Peter 5:8 Be sober, be vigilant, because your adversary the devil, like a roaring lion, walks about, seeking whom he may devour.

Consequences of backsliding

Psalm 106:15 "The Israelites wanted their own way. God gave them their way but sent a leanness into their soul.

Psalm 106:41 "God gave them into the hand of Satan, to rule over them.

Psalms 78: 49 "He cast upon them the fierceness of His anger, wrath and indignation and trouble by sending evil angels among them.

Ezk. 18:24 "When the righteous turns away from His righteousness and commits iniquity, shall he live? All his righteousness that he had shall not be mentioned."

II Peter 2:20, 21 "For if after they tasted the good of the Lord they return to their sinful ways, the latter end will be worse than the beginning. For it had been better for them not to have known the way of righteousness, after they have known it, to turn from the holy commandment delivered unto them."

II Peter 2:22 "But it is happened unto them according to the true proverb, the dog is turned to his own vomit again; and the sow that was washed, to her wallowing in the mire."

Jer. 3:14" God is married to the backslider."

Jer. 3:22 "Return and I will heal your backsliding, saith the Lord.

"Leanness"

Psalm 106:15 "God gave the Israelites their way but he sent a leanness into their soul."

Ever since Adam's sin in the Garden of Eden the depravity of man has manifested. Man has floundered in his rebellion, wanting his rebellion, wanting his own way, forgetting God. But not without a price as leanness has crept in, causing man to suffer in many ways.

What is Leanness?

1. Having no fear of the Lord.
2. Experiencing poverty.
3. Bad habits.
4. People on welfare.
5. People running excessively to doctors.
6. People excessively taking pills.
7. People on alcohol and drugs.
8. Priorities all screwed up.
9. Curses are handed down.
10. Ungodly music.
11. Husband: No leadership.
12. No family prayer.
14. No tradition (Family holidays etc.)
15. No budgeting.
16. No planning for the future.
17. No discipline.
18. Pride.
19. No paying tithes.
20. No regular Church attendance.

But we have good news!! Jesus Christ came to redeem (restore-repurchase-buy back) that which was lost!! Not only to restore fellowship with the Father, but get delivered from all the garbage that sin has caused. Solution: Seek truth!! Jesus Christ left a legacy that man may follow to acquire the abundant life that He promised to all believers.

       1.) Water baptism
       2.) B.H.S. (Baptism of the Holy Spirit)
       3.) Discipleship (soldiering), put on armor, break curses, pick up cross. (Deliverance)
       4.) Take authority over the enemy.

The Solar System

1. Six billion miles across (6,000,000,000)

2. Milky Way (our galaxy) 4 Billion stars...Psalm 147:4...God knows the names of each star.

3. Nearest star: 26,000,000,000,000 (Trillion) miles away.

4. There are 100 billion galaxies like the Milky Way.

5. 1,480,000 million, million, million planets & satellites in space.

6. 360,000 million, million, million major planets in the vast solar system.

How great is our God! How great is His name! Big enough to rule the universe yet small enough to live within our hearts!

The hard sayings of Jesus

As we read the word of God, we run across many sayings of Jesus that really is hard for us to comprehend. Not until we learn the truth of Jesus' teachings can we begin to understand and what He is illustrating in these sayings. What then is truth? First of all truth "is" Jesus (John 14:6) "I am the way, the truth and the life"

Second of all Jesus did not come to this earth for the sole purpose to take you and I to heaven but to take back that which was lost! What was lost? What was lost was the intimacy that Adam had with God before the fall.

Jesus came to do the Father's will. The will of the Father for Jesus was to drive out the "depraved nature" so that man would be capable to receive the Father's love. He taught the disciples first His "Kingdom of God theory," as examples, now He's teaching us!!

1. Mark 9:1...Jesus: "Some of you standing here will not see death until you have seen the "Kingdom of God" come in power." **Note!** Jesus was talking about the Kingdom of God within you. (The "Dunamis" Power found in the Baptism in the Holy Spirit).

2. Luke 9:23...Jesus: "Let Him deny himself, take up His cross and follow me." **Note!** Again, Jesus is referring to the process of losing the old nature and taking on the Jesus nature. That's why we are instructed to put off and put on. (Eph. 4:20-27) (Col. 3:8-15).

3. Matt. 10:34 Jesus: "I come not to send peace, but a sword on the earth." **Note!** Jesus was informing His disciples of the task that lay ahead for them. There would be people who would become their enemies because of a stand for him. Sword = controversy, striving, fighting. (Strong's Concordance.)

4. Matt. 12:28-31, Mark 3:27-29 Jesus: "Blasphemy against the Holy Spirit." **Note!** The subject here was deliverance (out with the old nature) it is a serious thing to make mockery of the ministry of Jesus Christ!

5. Matt. 16:23 Jesus: "Get thee behind me Satan."
Note! Peter had just replied to Jesus "You don't need to be killed!" Jesus addressed Him, not to Peter but to the demon speaking thru Peter using his vocal cords. Jesus said "Get thee behind me Satan."

6. Luke 10:18 Jesus: "I saw Satan fall from heaven as lighting."
Note! The 70 disciples returned saying "the demons had to obey us!" Jesus stated: "I saw Satan's kingdom coming down," rejoicing in His spirit. His ultimate plan for man was being activated. (I Cor. 4:20) (Matt. 12:28) (Luke 17:21) (Acts 20:25) (Matt. 10:5-8) (Acts 1:8).

God's will for man

As we look at the scriptures we find that God has a plan for the restoration of man. Every step in His plan for restoration is centered around the Lord Jesus. From Jesus to the least of the brethren everyone was to do the "will of God." In order for a smooth operation it was necessary for the participation of both God and man.

Jesus emptied himself of His deity and became an example for His followers. John 5:30 (Jesus) "I seek not my own will, but the will of my Father who sent me."

Luke 22:42 Jesus in the Garden of Gethsemane before His crucifixion. "Father, if it be your will, remove this cup from me. Nevertheless, not my will, but yours be done."

Matt. 7:21 "Not everyone that saith unto me, Lord, Lord shall enter the Kingdom of heaven, but he that doeth that will of my father which is in Heaven. "

John 9:31 God hears not sinners, but those who worship Him and do His will, those He hears.

John 7:17 "If any man will do my doctrine, he will be doing the will of my Father."

Matt. 12:50 "For whosoever shall do the will of my Father, the same is my brother, sister and mother."

Romans 12:2 Be not conformed to this world, but be ye transformed by the **"Renewing of your mind"** That ye may prove what is the good, and acceptable, and perfect will of God.

Soul...mind, will and emotions.

III John 2 Beloved, I wish above all things that thou mayest prosper and be in health, even as they soul prospereth.

Jesus
His Humanity
Son of God – Son of Man

Jesus Christ of Nazareth came to the earth to be our savior, our healer, our deliverer and our example. The question arises, how could Jesus be our example, He was God in the flesh? He was sinless; He didn't have any curses to deal with, nor evil soul-ties.

John 1:1 The word (Jesus) was God.

John 1:14 The word was made flesh and dwelt among us.

Phil. 2:7 Jesus emptied himself, and stripped himself of all privileges and rightful dignity, taken on the form of a servant.

He started His ministry when He was baptized in the river Jordan, receiving the "Dunamis" power. (Luke 4)

Jesus was both the Son of God and the "Son of Man."

John 5:27 God hath given Him authority to execute judgment because He is the "Son of Man."

Demons did not want to call Jesus "The son of Man" Acts 7:56 Stephen as he was being stoned looked up and said, "I see the Son of Man standing at the right hand of God!" The demons in the people cried out with a loud voice, putting their hands over their ears and charged him and stoned him.

Chapter Six

The Ministry of Jesus Christ

In the Christian circles today we are hearing over and over again. John 8:31, 32 if you continue in my word you shall come to know the truth and the truth shall set you free!

The truth is Jesus Christ. John 14:6 I am the way the life and the truth. We forget Jesus was present when Adam sinned. He witnessed what sin did – how Satan became the god of this world, how curses came into focus how evil soul ties and the depravity of man came into focus.

Jesus started his ministry when he was 30 years of age starting with the 12 apostles then the 70 and now with us Mark 16:17

In order for the Christian to experience some heat of the intimacy that Adam had with God. The old Adamic nature that we inherited needs to be driven out.

Satan and his cohorts (demons) will not budge unless force is used. Luke 10:19

Jesus: behold I give you power and authority to tread upon serpents and scorpions and nothing by any means hurt you.

That's why Jesus came to launch his discipleship program. He came to form an army! Why? Because there's a war on! Receiving Christ as your savoir is the pistol shot that starts the race. God is Love! So full of love, he is looking for someone to express it through the ministry of Jesus Christ His only begotten son. We Christians start shedding the old nature; little by little we are changed.

Jesus came as our savoir, our healer, our deliver and our example. He is our plumbline (Amos 5) A plumbline is a carpenter's tool that gives you a straight line.

Important references for the Ministry of Jesus Christ

Jesus Doctrine

It is important that we understand the Doctrine of Jesus Christ. The King James Version reveals this in a very unique way.

1. Mark 1:22 They were astonished at His Doctrine. What was Jesus' Doctrine? Jesus' Doctrine was the Kingdom of God. Mark 1:14, 15

2. Mark 1:23-26 The man in the synagogue was delivered of an unclean spirit.

3. Mark 1:27 They said: What new Doctrine (1322) is this?

4. Mark 4:2 Jesus said unto them (In His Doctrine) (1322)

5. Mark 4:11 Jesus: Unto you it is given to know the mystery of the Kingdom of God

6. Mark 11:18 All the people were astonished at His Doctrine. (1322)

7. Acts 2:41 They that received the word that Peter preached, were baptized and about 3,000 souls were saved. Acts 2:42 And they continued   steadfastly in the Apostles Doctrine. (1322).

8. Luke 4:32 They were astonished at His Doctrine for His word was with power Luke 4:33 Jesus cast an evil spirit out of the man in the synagogue.

9. John 7:17 If any man do His will, he shall know the Doctrine. (1322)

10. Rom. 16:17 Mark them which cause divisions contrary to the doctrine (1322) which ye have learned and avoid them.

11. II Tim. 4:3 For the time will come when they will not endure sound Doctrine!

12. II Tim. 4:2 Preach the word, reprove, rebuke and exhort with all long suffering and <u>Doctrine</u>. (1322)

13. I Tim. 1:3 They were instructed by <u>Paul not to teach no other Doctrine</u>.

14. If there comes any to your house and don't have the doctrine (1322) of Christ don't receive them!

What was the Apostles doctrine?

1. Matt. 10:1 Heal the sick-cast out devils

2. Luke 9:1 Heal the sick-cast out devils.

3. Luke 9:2 Preach the Kingdom of God.

4. I Cor. 4:20 For the Kingdom of God is not in word but in power.

Luke 4:43 Jesus: I must preach the Kingdom of God to other cities also.

Acts 8:12 Philip preached the Kingdom of God.

Acts 20:25 Paul preached the Kingdom of God.

The Epistles proclaim the Doctrine of Jesus Christ

1. I Tim. 1:3 (Paul) Charge some that they teach no other <u>Doctrine</u>.

2. I Tim. 4:13 (Paul) Till I come give attendance to reading, to exhortation and to <u>Doctrine</u>. (1319)

3. I Tim. 6:1 That the name of God and His <u>Doctrine</u> (1319) be not blasphemed.

4. I Tim. 6:3 If any man teach otherwise and consent not to wholesome words, even the words of our Lord Jesus Christ and to the <u>Doctrine</u> (1319) which is according to Godliness.

5. II Tim.4:2 Preach the word, be instant in season, out of season, reprove, rebuke and exhort with all longsuffering and <u>doctrine. (1322)</u>

6. II Tim.4:3 The time will come when they will not endure sound <u>Doctrine</u>. (1319)

7. Titus 1:9 Holding fast the faithful word as He has been taught that He may be able by <u>sound doctrine (1319)</u> both to exhort and to convince the gainsayers.

8. II John 1:9 Who so abideth not in the doctrine (1322) Hath not God.

9. II John 1:10 If there come unto you, and bring not this Doctrine (1322) receive Him not into your house, neither bid God's speed.

(I Thess. 5:21 Prove all things)
(Strong's) Doctrine =1322 Instruction, to teach.
Doctrine = 1319 Instruction, learning, teaching.

The Ministry of Jesus Christ

Jesus came to restore man's intimacy with God, not only to quicken man's spirit but heal the soul and the body. To drive out the carnal nature.

Spirit: Worship-Conscience-Intuition
Soul: Mind-will- emotions
Body: Bones-flesh-blood

1. Preach to the masses – spirit
2. Taught the disciples – soul
3. Cast out devils – soul
4. Healed the sick – body

Luke 4:43 Jesus came to preach the Kingdom of God.

A. John 3:17 For God did not send His son into the world to condemn the world but that the world through Him might be "saved." (Sozo)

B. Luke 9:56 For the Son of Man has not come to destroy men's lives, but to "save" (Sozo) them.

C. Luke 19:10 For the Son of Man has come to seek and to "Save" (Sozo) that which was lost.

"Sozo" = heal, deliver, make whole, (Strong's Concordance).

D. Phil. 2:12 Work out your "salvation" with fear and trembling!

"Salvation" = deliverance from bondages (Thayer's Lexicon)

I John 3:8 Jesus came to destroy the works of the devil!

God's complete plan of restoration

I Thess. 5:23 And the very God peace sanctify you "<u>wholly</u>," and I pray to God your "<u>whole</u>" spirit, soul and body be preserved "<u>blameless</u>" unto the coming of our Lord Jesus Christ.

"Wholly" 3651 (Strong's concordance) (Complete to the end).

"Whole" 3648 (Strong's Concordance) (Complete in every part) (Perfectly Sound – entire)

"Blameless" (Greek = "Amemptos") (Literally means without blemish or spot)

John 14:30 (Jesus) "The prince of this world has nothing on me." Purpose of discipleship...that we can get rid of the "old nature" that Satan would have no "legal rights" on us. Amen!!

The ministry of Jesus Christ
The early Church

As we observe the word of God we find that not only did Jesus give us an example with His life, but he also left an important procedure in which to follow, He started with the 12 disciples, then the 70 and now He has instructed the Church to follow the same pattern.

The early Church was powerful Church. They obtained the over coming victory that God has for the present day Church also. Jesus Christ is the same yesterday, today and forever. Jesus Christ laid down a legacy in which to follow. The early Church followed it! How? How did they do it?

Acts Chapter 5 expresses it completely!

1. Acts 5:3 Ananias and Saphira were found out by discernment. (By Peter) They were struck dead.

2. Acts 5:5, 11 Fear of the Lord followed.

3. Acts 5:12 Signs and wonders were present.

4. Acts 5:14 Results- many people were getting saved!

5. Acts 5:15 The sick were getting healed, even thru Peter's shadow!

6. Acts 5:16 Ministry of Jesus Christ: Unclean spirits were cast out!

7. Acts 5:18 apostles were beaten and thrown in jail.

8. Acts 5:19 The angel of the Lord opened the prison doors.

9. Acts 5:29 They were back on the street preaching Jesus.

10. Acts 5:40 They were beaten again!

11. Acts 5:41 Apostles "rejoiced" that they were worthy to suffer shame for the name of Jesus!

12. Acts 5:42 The apostles continued preaching and teaching the doctrine of Jesus Christ.

The Lord Jesus healed in many different ways

1. Without result being apparent at once.
   A. Luke 17:14 The ten Lepers. "Go show yourselves to the priests" **Note!** As they went, they were cleansed. (Healed)

2. Some were instantaneously healed.
   Matt. 15: 30, 31 Great multitudes came to Him, having with them those who were lame, blind, dumb etc. and he healed them all!

3. Indicated healing would come in the near future.
   John 9:7 Jesus put clay and anointed his eyes. Then He instructed him to go to the pool of Siloam and wash them out.

4. Sometimes first removed a man form his surroundings
   Mark 8:22, 23 Jesus led the blind man out of town.

5. All manner of diseases
   Matt. 4:23, 24 Jesus also healed all those who were afflicted with various diseases and those under the power of demons, and epileptic and those who were paralyzed.

6. Jesus healed by the touch and others touching Him.
   Matt. 8:3, Luke 8:44, Mark 1:31, Luke 6:10, Mark 7:34 Woman touched the hem of his garment. (Issue of blood stopped) Jesus put forth His hand and the leper was made clean.

7. Jesus healed from a distance.
   John 4:46-53 Nobleman's son

Matt. 15:22-28 Jesus cast the demon out of the Syrophenician Woman's daughter at a distance.

8. Jesus also healed chronic cases.
Matt. 9:20 Woman who was diseased with an issue of blood "twelve years."

Luke 13:11 Woman who had a spirit of infirmity of "eighteen years."

John 5:5 A man had an infirmity "Thirty eight years."

John 14:12 Verily, verily I say unto you, he that believeth on me, the works that I do ye shall do also.

Chapter Seven

Baptism in the Holy Ghost

When we receive Jesus Christ as Savoir we enlist in the Lord's Army. God would never call us into battle without equipping us with the power to accomplish the task. We are to overcome. Make no mistake, when Jesus commanded the people to go to the upper room, it was for a good reason. To give them power as we go to Strong's Concordance we find that the word Power found in John 1:12 is different than the word power in Acts 1:8

John 1:12.... As many as received Him (Jesus) to them gave He the "Power" to become the sons of God Power=Exousia (Strong 1411) Authority.

Act1:8...you shall receive "power" after the Holy Ghost is come upon you!

Power = (Dunamis) mighty works – violence (Strong's) When a person receives the B.H.S. He will be able to speak in a heavenly language. As it states in (Acts 2:4 "They spoke in tongues as the spirit gave them utterance!)

I remember years ago I went forward at the Duluth Gospel Tabernacle for the B.H.S. I didn't receive tongues at that time but a few days later I was in the kitchen of the fire station by myself. I made some utterance come out of my mouth & the spirit of the living God fell on me & I received. What a joy it was to speak in tongues. From that time on I received a hunger for God's word that won't quit.

I've taught spiritual warfare for many years & I've use that "dunamis power" to bind the enemy who's out to <u>steal</u> my inheritance, <u>kill</u> my joy & <u>destroy</u> my testimony!

Important references for Baptism in the Holy Spirit

It takes power to win a war

If a believer desires to be in the will of God he will come to the knowledge that God has called him to be a soldier. A soldier needs to acquire the tools to equip him to fulfill his calling. The believer needs power to be able to get the job done. He needs the baptism of the Holy Ghost. It is a command (Acts 1:4) The world "power" found in John 1:12 is different than the word "power" found in Acts 1:8. John 1:12 ...Greek (Exousia) means authority. Acts 1:8 ...Greek (dunamis) means violence, worker of miracles-abundance.

We are to do everything that will build us up in the Lord. I Corinthians 14:4...He that speaks in a heavenly language, "Edifies himself!" That's for "Every" BELIEVER. We need altar calls for it! I Tim. 2:3 Endure hardness as a good soldier of Jesus Christ. II Tim. 2:4 No man that warreth entangles himself with the affairs of this world, that he may please Him who has "chosen him to be a soldier."

Too many Christians are running up and down the sidelines with their clean uniforms on. It is time to get at the devil and see ourselves and our loved one's freed from the bondage that plagues us.

Nothing much gets accomplished unless some authority is used!

Benefits of the Baptism in the Holy Ghost in regards to healing

Acts 1:8 You shall receive power (1411 Dunamis) a Holy Ghost has come upon you.

1. Luke 5:17 and the power (1411 Dunamis) of the lord present to heal!

2. Luke 6:17-19 Virtue (1411 Dunamis) went out of Jesus healed them all!

3. Mark 5:30 Virtue (1411 Dunamis) went out of Jesus to the woman with the issue of blood when she touched the hem of His garment and she was healed!

4. Luke 9:1 Jesus gave the disciples power (1411 Dunamis) heal and cure diseases!

5. Matt. 10:1 Jesus gave His disciples power (1411 Dunamis) against unclean spirits, to cast them out, and to all manner of sickness and diseases!

John 14:12 Jesus: Verily, verily, I say unto you, the works that I do, ye shall do also!

The baptism in the Holy Ghost is a must for everyone.

Benefits of the Baptism in the Holy Ghost for a congregation

Jesus Christ came to set up a plan for the Church to become overcomers and acquire the abundant life. The baptism in the Holy Spirit is needed to reach that goal.

When we look at scripture we find that the world "power" found in John 1:12 (Exausia) is different than the word "power" in acts 1:8. (Dunamis)

1. The congregation needs the B.H.S. For holy boldness.
   Acts 4:31 They were filled with the Holy Ghost and spoke the word with "boldness".

2. The congregation needs the B.H.S. to overcome fear.
   II Timothy 1:7 Paul exhorts Timothy: God has not given you a spirit of fear but: Power (Dunamis) love and a sound mind!

3. The Congregation needs the B.H.S. to reach maturity.
   Romans 1:16 The apostle Paul states "I am not ashamed of the Gospel of Jesus Christ, for it is the "Power" of God unto Salvation". (Greek = Sozo)

Bible: A book of warfare

Military terminology is used frequently in the New Testament.

1. Protection is seen in "armor of God." (Ehp. 6:11)
2. The word of God is compared to a "sword." (Heb. 4:12)
3. Satan's attacks are called "Fiery darts." (Eph. 6:16)
4. Faith is referred to as "The good fight." (I Tim. 6:12
5. Believers are told to "war a good warfare." (I Tim. 1:18)
6. "Be sober, be vigilant because your adversary the devil walks about seeking whom he man devour!" (I Peter 5:8)

We need the baptism in the Holy Ghost

1. **For Holy Boldness:**
   Acts 4:31 "They were all filled with the Holy Ghost and spoke the word of God with boldness.

2. **To overcome fear:**
   II Tim. 1:17 God hath not given to you a spirit of fear, but of <u>power, (Dunamis)</u> love and a sound mind.

3. **To reach maturity:**
   Romans 1:16 (Paul0 I am not ashamed of the gospel of Jesus Christ for it is the <u>power (Dunamis)</u> that worketh in us.

4. **To allow God's input:**
   Eph. 3:20 He is able to do exceedingly above all we ask of think, according to the <u>power (Dunamis)</u> that worketh in us.

5. **To help us endure suffering:**
   Acts 9:16, 17 (Paul) Ananias laid hands on Paul for the baptism in the Holy Ghost. (Jesus to Ananias) for I will show him how great things he must suffer for my name's sake.

6. **To become over-comers:**
   Preaching of the cross unto us which are saved it is the <u>power (Dunamis)</u> of God.

7. **To warfare against the enemy:**
   Acts (6:8-10 (Stephen) Stephen, full of Faith and power (Dunamis) did great wonders and miracles and they were not able to resist the wisdom and the spirit by which he spoke.

8. **To promote healing:**
   Mark 5: 28-30 The woman with the issue of blood touched the hem of Jesus' garment and <u>virtue (Dunamis)</u> went out of him and she was healed. (Jesus received the B.H.S. at the Jordan River)

9. To obtain a good measure of hope:

Romans 15:13 Now may the God of hope, fill you with all joy and peace in believing, that ye may abound in hope, through the <u>power</u> (Dunamis) of the Holy Ghost

10. Able to preach the kingdom of God:

Luke 4:43 Jesus preached the Kingdom of God.
I Cor. 4:20 The kingdom of God is not in word, but in <u>power</u>. (Dunamis)

Note! Those who have received the Baptism in the Holy Ghost are more able to preach the Kingdom of God.

John 1:12 To as many as received Him, to them gave He the power (exousia) to become the sons of God.

Acts 1:8 You shall receive power (Dunamis) after that the Holy Ghost has come upon you.

Exousia = 1849 Strong's concordance = authority, jurisdiction, right.

Dunamis=1411 Strong's=miraculous power, abundance, violence, worker of miracles.

Where does it say?

Many times in your walk with the Lord you are asked: Why do you believe the way you do and where is it found in scripture?

1. Where does it say: We are to do the works of Jesus? John 14:12, John 17:18, John 20:21, Rev. 3:21.

2. Where does it say: The Baptism in the Holy Ghost is a separate experience. Acts 1:8, Acts 9:17, Acts 19:6

3. Where does it say: Where Jesus stated "Go and make Disciples?" Matt. 28:19, Matt. 28:20 Teach them what I have commanded you. What did He command? Matt. 10:5-8

4. Where does it say: A believer can have an evil spirit?
   A. Luke 14:12, 13 The woman with a spirit of infirmity.
   B. Mark 5:6 The Gadarene.
   C. Matt. 15:20-28 The Syrophenician woman.
   D. Acts 8:3-8 Philip's preaching in Samaria.
   E. Mark 1:23-26 The man in Church.

5. Where does it say: That speaking in tongues is the evidence of the Baptism in the Holy Ghost? Acts 10:44-46, Acts 2:4

6. Where does it say: That the soul is the mind, will and emotions?
   A. Deut. 11:18 We store God's word with our soul. (Mind).
   B. Deut. 6:5 We love the Lord with our soul. (Will).
   C. Psalm 142:7 We praise the Lord with our soul (Emotions).

7. Where does it say: To seek the kingdom of God first? Matt. 6:33

8. Where does it say: Jesus preached the Kingdom of God? Luke 4:43

9. Where does it say: We are to love the Lord and hate evil? Psalm 97:10

10. Where does is say: The Israelites are our example? I Cor. 10:11

11. Where does is say: He who does not pick up His cross "daily," and follow me, cannot be my disciple? Luke 9:23, Luke 14:27

12. Where does it say: The purpose of Jesus' ministry? I John 3:8, Luke 19:10, John 10:10, John 3:17

13. Where does it say: To put on the armour? Eph. 6:13-17

14. Where does it say: God has called you to be a soldier? II Tim. 2:3, 4

15. Where does it say: If any lack wisdom, let him ask God? James 1:5

Where in the Bible does it mention the Baptism in the Holy Ghost?

1. Acts 2:4 Upper room: They were all filled with the Holy Ghost and spoke in tongues as the spirit gave them utterance.

2. Acts 4:33 The early Church received the B. H. S. for holy boldness.

3. Acts 8:14 Peter and John laid their hands on the Gentiles and they received the Holy Ghost.

4. Acts 19:6 The Apostle Paul laid hands on them and they spoke in tongues and prophesied.

Why Tongues?

1. Praise: I Cor. 14:15 I will sing with the understanding and I will sing with the spirit.

2. Building up oneself: Jude 1:20 but ye beloved building up yourselves on your most holy faith praying in the Holy Ghost.

3. Edify oneself: I Cor. 14:4 Speaking in tongues edifies oneself.

4. Evidence of the baptism in the Holy Ghost: Acts 10:46 They knew they had received the B.H.S. for they heard them speak in tongues and magnify God.

Chapter Eight

Building a Foundation

In Matt 7:24-27 we have the parable of "The House on the Rock" when the rains came, and the winds blew and beat upon the house it fell not! For it was founded on a rock! I called the superior library and asked the librarian if she could get me some information why the palm tree could withstand the 100 MPH hurricanes. She came back and informed me of the strong "root-system" it has, and also it bends way over. We need to be pliable! **Note!** We need to bend and be teachable so we can stand and not faint. It's pliable. Psalm 92:12 The righteous shall flourish like a palm tree. Listen, the winds of adversity are going to increase in these closing days for the believer. We need a good "Root system" (Foundation) I don't believe a Christian can overcome much unless he gets the right "mind-set"! It will cause him to put on his armour, pick up his cross and present his body a living sacrifice <u>before</u> he starts his day. By doing so gets him on the right frequency. He will be able to hear the Lord's still voice and find direction for his life. Isa. 26:3 Thou will keep him in perfect peace, whose mind is stayed on thee.

The spiritual battle is won or lost in the battlefield of the mind! It's up to the believer to take steps in cleaning up his thought life! When a negative thought comes into the mind the believer hop on it like a rooster on a June bug. He needs to cast it down and refuse to accept it. (II Cor. 10:5 Casting down imaginations) Take authority over the thought, command it to go to "Dry places" take a couple coughs. (Matt. 12:43)

Important references for Building a Foundation

Salvation: An ongoing Revelation

1. Phil. 2:12 "Work out your salvation" with fear and trembling. Salvation = soteria (Greek) bring to completion. Deliverance from all bondages. (Thayers Lexicon).

2. Rom. 1:16 For I am not ashamed of the gospel of Jesus Christ, for it is the power (Dunamis) of God." "Unto Salvation."

3. Heb. 7:25 He is able to save them to the "Uttermost." Uttermost (Strong's) = complete-entire-whole.

4. I Thess. 5:23 The very God of peace sanctify you "Wholly," and I pray your "Whole" spirit, soul and body be preserved "Blameless." (Saved) (Wholly) = 3651 Strong's concordance – "Complete to the end." (Whole) = 3648 Strong's – "Complete in every part" perfectly sound – entire. (Blameless) = Greek "Amemptos" Without blemish or spot.

5. II Tim. 3:15 The Holy word of God that is able to make thee wise "unto salvation."

6. John 1:12 To as many as received him, to them gave he power "To become the sons of God." (It's the pistol shot that starts the race.)

7. Titus 2:14 Jesus gave himself of that He might "redeem" us form all iniquity, to purify unto himself a peculiar people. "Redeem" = Repurchase=buyback-to rescue- to reclaim.

One of the biggest deceptions Satan has been able to pull off against the Church is that salvation is just receiving Jesus Christ as savior. This is good, but it is far form the purpose of Jesus' coming. Jesus came to make disciples (Soldiers). He came to redeem that which was lost! If we acquired everything at salvation, then we wouldn't need to be transformed by the "Renewing of the mind." (Rom. 12:2)

The baptism in the Holy Ghost is given to become a witness, not only to and witness. The dunamis power is given to drive out the old Adamic Nature and obtain the Power of righteousness.

Unrighteous vs. Righteous

In the world we have seen many wars take place. Bitter hatred between nations bloody wars that know no peace agreements. But none can compare with the war that's taken place in the spiritual realm. Satan knows his time is short and he's unleashing many legions of demons in an attempt to block the Christian soldier of accomplishing God's will for their lives.

1. I John 3:13 Marvel not my brethren, if the world hates you.

2. Psalm 37:12 The wicked plotteth against the just and he gnasheth his teeth.

3. Galatians 5:17 the flesh lusted against the spirit and the spirit against the flesh.

4. Luke 6:22 Blessed are ye when men hate you, separate from you and reproach you.

5. John 17:14 Jesus: The world hateth my disciples because they are not of this world.

6. II Cor. 2:14, 15 The unsaved cannot stand the aroma around the righteous.

7. Matt. 24:9 They shall deliver you up to be afflicted and shall kill you and ye shall be hated of all nations for my name's sake!

8. Prov. 19:10 The blood thirsty hateth the upright.

9. Luke 21:17 Ye shall be hated for my name's sake.

10. Matt. 10:22 And ye shall be hated for my name's sake; but he that endureth to the end shall be saved. **Note!** The people feared Jesus because He was a righteous man. His very presence convicted them of their sins. The same with God's people.

11. Mark 6:20 King Herod feared John knowing he was a holy and just man.

12. I Sam. 18:12 King Saul was afraid of David because the Lord was with Him.

13. Exodus 12:35, 36 The Egyptians feared the Israelites and even lent to them.

Why is righteousness so important?

1. II Sam. 22:21 The Lord rewarded me "According to my righteousness;" according to the cleanness of my hands.

2. Isaiah 54:17 No weapon formed against me shall prosper. Why? Because of "my righteousness."

3. Romans 14:17 The Kingdom of God is "Righteousness," peace, and joy in the Holy Ghost, **Note!** The joy of the Lord is your strength. It comes from the peace you receive when you become righteous. Righteousness First, peace second, then joy in the Holy Ghost!

4. Psalm 7:8 We are judged according to "our righteousness!"

5. Psalm 37:29 The "Righteous" shall inherit the land.

6. Psalm 34:15 The eyes of the Lord are on the "righteous" his ears are open to their cry!

7. Psalm 37:39 The salvation of the "righteous" is of the Lord, He is their strength in time of trouble. Psalm 37:40 he will help them and deliver them, the "righteous" trust in the Lord.

8. Psalm 37:30 The mouth of the "righteous" speaks wisdom. Psalm 37:31 He has the word of his God in his heart. None of his steps shall slide

9. Proverbs 10:11 The "Righteous man's" Mouth is a well of life.

10. Psalm 37:21 A "Righteous" man shows mercy and gives of himself.

11. Hebrews 12:11 The Lord blesses those who embrace chastening, with "Righteousness!"

12. Rom. 6:16 Know ye not, to whom you yield yourself to obey whether sin unto death or obedience unto "righteousness."
The purpose of discipleship is gain the power of "righteousness" John 14:30 Jesus: "Satan has nothing on me!" (Our example)

Walk with the Lord (Daily)

1. Luke 11:3 Give us this day our daily bread.

2. Prov. 8:34 Blessed is the man that heareth me, watching daily at my gates.

3. Luke 9:23 if any man come after me, let him deny himself and take up his cross daily and follow me.

4. Lam. 3:22 The Lord's mercies are new every morning.

5. Heb. 3:13 But exhort one another daily lest any of you be hardened through the deceitfulness of sin.

6. Psalm 145:2 Lord, everyday I will bless thee.

7. Psalm 96:2 Sing unto the Lord, bless His name, show forth his salvation from day to day.

8. Deut. 30:15 See, saith God, I have set before thee this day, life and good, and death and evil.

9. Joshua 24:15 Choose you this day, who you are going to serve.

10. II Cor. 4:16 through our outward man perish, yet the inward man is renewed daily.

11. Acts 5:42 The early Church met daily in the temple, teaching and preaching Jesus Christ.

12. Psalm 86:3 Be merciful unto me O' Lord, for I cry unto thee daily

13. Psalm 88:9 Lord, I have called unto thee daily.

14. Psalm 68:19 God blesses us daily with benefits.

15. Psalm 61:8 I will sing praises unto thy name forever, that I may daily perform my vows.

16. Exodus 16:4 The Lord rained manna on His people daily. John 6:32 Jesus is the bread of life (our manna) The word of God states that this war with the enemy is fought on a daily basis.

17. Psalm 91:5 Reveals that the enemies arrows are flying at us daily. Therefore: Put on the armor daily, Pick up your cross daily, present yourself a living sacrifice to God daily.

Walk in the spirit

Apostle Paul: (Gal. 5:16) This I say then, walk in the spirit, and ye shall not fulfill the lusts of the flesh.

What does it mean to walk in the spirit?

As a soldier of the Lord we are to live our life on a daily basis, to take one day at a time with our mind stayed on the Lord. Jesus went around doing good and healing all who were oppressed of the devil. (Acts 10:38)

1. **Put on the armour (Eph 16:13-17).**
   John 10:10 You have an enemy who is out to destroy you.

2. **Speak positive (Proverbs 18:21).**
   Life and death are in the power of the tongue.

3. **Crucify the flesh!**
   Take up your cross daily! (Luke 9:23, 24) put off the old nature, put on the new. Break old habit patterns.

4. **Stay in the scriptures.**
   (Psalm 119:11) They word have I hid in my heart that I might not sin against thee O' Lord.

5. **Develop a life of praise and prayer.**
   (Psalm 71:8) Let my mouth be filled with they praise and with thy honour all day long.

6. **Keep in touch with like believers. (Fellowship is a must!)**
   (Mal. 3:16) A special book of remembrance was made for those who met and shared Jesus Christ.

7. **Commit yourself totally to Christ. (Josh. 24:15)**
   "Choose you this day whom ye will serve." (Make that commitment each day.) Start in the morning, seek God's

leading in what He would have you do this day. Determine that every thought, word and action will reflect the very nature of Jesus Christ.

8. Pay tithes.

(Malt. 3:8-10) Bring all the tithes into the storehouse, prove me and see if I won't open the windows of heaven, and pour you out a blessing, that there shall not be room enough to receive it.

Obedience

1. **Obedience is a conformation you love God.**

   A. Jesus is our example John 14:30 The prince of this world
      has nothing on me. (Why didn't Satan have anything
      on Jesus?) John 14:31 (Jesus) Because I have obeyed
      the Father's commandments as a confirmation "I love
      Him"
   B. Jesus: our example (John 15:10 "If ye keep my
      commandments, ye shall abide in my love, even as I
      have kept my Father's commandments and abide in His
      love.

2. **Obedience purifies the soul.**

   A. Peter 1:22 By obeying the truth which leads to the love of
      the brethren.
   B. Psalm 41:4 Disobedience injures the soul—obedience
      heals the soul.

3. **Obedience leads to righteousness.**

   A. Romans 6:16 You are servants to whom you obey,
      whether sin unto death or of obedience unto
      righteousness

4. **Obedience prolongs your life**

   A. I Kings 3:14 If you will walk in my ways, keep my statues
      as thy father David, I will lengthen thy days.
   B. Prov. 4:10 Hear and receive my sayings and thy years of
      they life will be many.

5. **Obedience in tithing.**

   A. Mal, 4:10 By paying tithes God will rebuke the devourer
      for you. God will pour out blessings.

6. Obedience brings on prosperity

A. I Kings 2:3 Keep the charge of the Lord, walk in His ways, keep His statues, His commandments and His judgments and His testimonies that you may prosper in all that you do.
B. Deut. 29:9 Keep therefore the words of this covenant and "do them," that ye may prosper in all that you do. Heb. 5:8 Jesus learned obedience by the things that He suffered.

John 15:10 "If you obey ye shall abide in God's love.

John 15:11 The result: brings on joy!

I John 5:2 Obeying God is the key to loving the brethren.

I John 4:21 Love God/ Love the brethren.

Perseverance

Eph. 6:12 We "wrestle" against principalities and powers.

1. Gen. 32:26 (Jacob) "I will not let you go except you bless me"! All night Jacob wrestled with the angel. His perseverance paid off.

2. Luke 19:2 (Zacchaeus) Nothing was going to stop him from seeing Jesus! Zacchaeus could not see Jesus coming because of his height. He climbed a tree. Result: Jesus saw him and spent the day at his house!

3. Mark 2:4 (Man lowered through the roof) The house was filled with people, but that did not stop them. Jesus rewarded their faith and persistence. Result: The man received his healing!

4. Matt. 15:27 (Syrophenician woman) result: Her daughter was delivered!
Jesus words to her were to draw out her depth of faith. Saying "Deliverance is the children's bread." She called him "Lord" and because of her faith Jesus said: "Woman great is your faith"! Matt 15:23 The woman had continued to cry out to Jesus, so much so that the disciples asked Jesus to send her away. She was persistent and with her faith.

Jesus at first said "Deliverance is the children's bread: She called him "Lord" and because of her persistence she got her way. Jesus said: "Woman, great is your faith"!

5. Luke 22:44 (Jesus) at the Garden of Gethsemane Because of His love for mankind, "He persevered" so that the Father's will would be fulfilled.

6. Acts 12:5 (Peter in prison) the brethren's prayers released him! "Persevering prayer" was made for Peter at the house.

Result: God sent an angel to unshackle and lead him out of prison.

7. Mark 10:46 (Bartimaeus) Bartimaeus "persevered" Result: Received his sight! He would not listen to the crowd saying "sit down blind man" but continued on to Jesus who was coming down the road.

8. Phil. 5:14 (Paul) "I press toward the mark of the high calling of God!" Through all of Paul's trails and tribulations he did not fail to fulfill God's will for his life. "He persevered."

9. Luke 18:1 (Widow and the judge)
Because of her "persistence" she got her way!

10. Matt. 11:12 (The violent) take it by force!
Violent = 'To press" with courage and holy boldness.

Present your body a living sacrifice

There are two things that are important in the Christian's obedient walk with the Lord. One is that he is to work with God, and two, he is to do it on a daily basis. Presenting his body as a living sacrifice is a must to be led by the Holy Spirit for the day.

1. Be not conformed to this world
   II Peter 1:4 that we might be partakers of the divine nature.

2. Love without hypocrisy
   Matt. 5:43-44 Love you enemies, bless them.

3. Cleave to that which is good
   Acts 10:38 Jesus went about doing good.
   Eph. 2:10 We are created for good works.
   Gal. 6:9 Do not grow weary of well doing.

4. Be kindly affectionate one to another
   Titus 2:14 Jesus gave himself that he might purify Himself a peculiar people, zealous of good works. (We are created for good works) Matt. 25:36 I was sick and you visited me, in prison and you came to me. etc

5. Be not slothful in business
   Co. 3:22 Servants, obey your masters, not only in eye service but in duty, fearing Do.

6. Be fervent in sprit
   Fervent= to be hot! Deeply earnest, on fire for God!

7. Rejoice in the hope of the Lord
   Rom. 15:13 Now may the God of Hope, fill you with all peace and joy in believing that you may abound in hope, in the power of the Holy Ghost.

8. Be patient in tribulation
   Rom. 5:3 Glory in tribulations, tribulation worketh patience.

9. Continuing instant in prayer
    Live in fervent prayer to God.

10. Helping the saints
    Gal. 6:9 Do not grow weary of well doing. "So much more to the household of faith." Heb. 10:24 Provoke to love and good works.

11. Bless them that persecute you (Luke 6:28)
    Cry out to the Lord to give you strength in this area. Do not accuse the person, but the demonic force behind it. Cultivate a hatred for the devil. Forgive that person and place a blessing on him. (Be like Christ).

12. Rejoice with them that rejoice-weep with them that weep. Always be open to lend a helping hand, be sensitive to people.

13. Pay back not evil for evil
    This is a time to take stock of yourself, how far you've come in your walk.

14. When your enemy hungers-feed him!
    Luke 6:35 do good to your enemies, even lend to them.

15. Overcome evil with good
    This is the ultimate goal of Jesus' discipleship program, to change your nature to His nature. The way will not be easy, there will be tears, there will be sufferings, but there will also be the joy of the Lord. Amen!

Transformation
Old nature to new nature
Put off—put on process

The main thrust of the ministry of Jesus Christ is that we not only are converted but that we are transformed into the nature of Jesus Christ. That the intimacy with the Father can be restored. "It is essential that we work with the Lord in this process of shedding that old nature." Not only are we instructed to put on the armour each day but also to "put off the old and put on the new." Slowly but surely the power of righteousness will manifest in the soldier of the Lord.

DAILY PROCESS FOR CHANGING NATURE

PUT OFF

PUT ON

1. Eph. 4:22 Put off concerning the former conversation, the old man, which is corrupt according to the deceitful lusts.

2. Ephesians 4:24 And that you put on the new man, which after God is created in righteousness and true holiness.

3. Rom. 13:12 Let us cast off the works of darkness and let us put on the armour of light.

4. Col. 3:8 Put off all these: anger, wrath, malice, blasphemy and filthy communication.

5. Col. 3:12 Put on: Holiness, bowels of mercies, kindness, humbleness of mind, meekness and long suffering.

6. Col. 13:12 Put on: and above all these things, put on love which is the bond of perfect-ness.

Rom. 13:14 Put ye on the Lord Jesus Christ and make no provision for the flesh, to fulfill the lusts thereof!

God's forgiveness

Strange as it may seem, there are a lot of Christians that cannot comprehend the forgiveness of God. The enemy comes to condemn, accuse, putting a guilt trip on the child of God, robbing him of the peace that God has for him. They as "how can God forgive me after what I've done?" That thought needs to be rebuked and put under the blood.

What does God's word say?

I John 1:9 If you confess your sins, he is faithful to forgive you and cleanse you form all unrighteousness.

Phil. 3:13 (Paul) This "one thing" I do, forgetting those things which are behind, and reaching forth for those things which are before. (**Note!** Paul would not allow the enemy to condemn him in any way of His sins against the Church and personal sins.) He was going on, cleansed by the blood of Jesus!

1. Psalm 103:12 As far as the east is from the west He has removed our transgressions.

2. Micah 7:19 He will cast "all" of our sins into the depths of sea.

3. Isa. 43:25 I will blot out thy transgressions and remember their sins no more.

4. Jer. 31:34 I will forgive their iniquity and remember their sins no more!

5. Heb. 8:12 I will remember their sins no more.

6. Heb. 10:17 Their sins and iniquities I will remember no more.

7. Psalm 85:2 Thou has forgiven thy iniquity of they people, thou hast covered "all" their sins.

Note! Do not allow the enemy to put condemnation on you for past sins. When you confess them God will not only forgive you but also forget them! Selah.

If you have received prayer for this onslaught of the enemy and it still persists, then bind it to the authority of the third heaven and command it to loose its hold on you. Come against it and do not give up until it leaves you. It's time to get mad at the devil!

God's Protection

Psalm 103:2 Bless the Lord, O my soul, and forget not this benefits.

All through the scriptures we are reminded time and again the benefits that God has for those who love him and obey him. He does not want robots, but those believers who will work with him in the process of changing their nature. The believers who are willing to put on the armour, pick up their cross and present their bodies a living sacrifice each day. God wants back what Satan stole (intimacy with man) and he needs man's input to accomplish this through spiritual warfare. Benefits will come to those individuals. One of the benefits is the protection that God has for those who love and obey him.

1. Job 1:10 God put a hedge around Job's house and around his family. We are living in a day when we are seeing many tragedies taking place, even in the schools. We can ask God to put a hedge around our children too. If He did it for Job he will do it for you, He is no respecter of persons.)

2. Psalm 91:11 He shall give His angels charge over thee, to keep thee in all your ways. (Ask the Lord to have His angels put a hedge of protection around your loved ones or your children as you send them off to school.)

3. Psalm 34:7 The angel of the Lord encampeth round about them that fear him. Heb. 1:14 Are they not all ministering spirits (angels) sent forth to minister for them who are heirs of salvation.

4. Hosea 2:6 God put a hedge of thorns around Gomer (Hosea's wife) and made a wall around her. His wife returned to him, because of the promptings of the Holy Spirit. (We too can ask the lord to put a hedge of thorns around our wayward loved ones).

5. Zech. 2:5 For I saith the Lord will be unto her (Jerusalem) a wall of fire around and will be the Glory in the midst of her. (We too can ask the Lord to put a wall of fire around an area, or a meeting and clear out all hindering spirits etc.)

Chapter Nine

Spiritual warfare

SATAN

1. A real person (I peter 5:8 Because your enemy walketh about.)

2. Jesus dealt with him as a real person. (Luke 4:1-13)

3. Jesus waged war on satan. (As a real person) Luke 13:16 (Whom Satan hath bound.)

4. Teachings of Jesus Christ revealed satan as real person.
   Rev. 20:1-10 (The angel grabbed hold of satan and threw him in a pit.)

5. Personal conversation is carried on with him.
   Jude 9 Michael (The archangel) contended with the devil.

6. Personal descriptions are given to him.
   Full of wisdom...perfect in beauty.

7. Personal names...Lucifer-serpent-dragon-tempter-adversary- prince of this word-god of this world.

8. Satan has been seen with a body.
   Matt. 4:1-11 Jesus was tempted by him.
   Rev. 20:1 The angel grabbed him.
   Was bound bodily with chain and cast into prison.

9. Satan has a:
> A. Heart Isa. 14:13 For thou hast said in thine heart.
>
> B. Pride Ezek. 28:17 For though hast said thine heart
was lifted up because of thine beauty.
>
> C. Power Job 1:6-22 To do what he did to Job.
> Acts 26:18 (Paul) I turned from the power of satan unto
> God.
>
> D. Desires Luke 22:31 (Jesus) Simon, satan hath
desired to sift you as wheat.
>
> E. Lusts John 8:44 Ye are of your Father the devil and
the lusts of your Father ye will do.
>
> F. Speech Job 1:7 And satan said unto the Lord.

Important references for Spiritual Warfare

Spiritual warfare

When we read the word of God we find out that the whole Bible is a book of warfare. After what happened in the Garden of Eden and Adam's sin. God declared war on Satan (Gen. 3:15).

This part of the word is where the doctrine of Christ is first mentioned. Not only would God provide the cost of redemption thru His son Jesus but thru Jesus' doctrine would the battle be waged!

A lot is mentioned in the Gospels as well as the epistles about the doctrine of Jesus Christ. It's important that we search it out.

John 7:17 If any man will do his will know the doctrine! (I guess it must be important!) Mark 1:21, 22 They were astonished at his doctrine! Mark 1:23 Deliverance was done in Church with Jesus casting out evil spirits

II Tim. 4:2 apostle Paul exhorted Pastor Timothy to "Preach the word, reprove, rebuke and exhort with all longsuffering and "Doctrine".

Note! A pastor's duty is awesome when we see what the Lord expects of them. They even have a different judgment.

James 3:1 (NKJ) My brethren let not many of you become teachers, knowing that we shall receive a stricter judgment!

Spiritual warfare II

Isn't it strange that Mary Magdalene was first to see Jesus after His resurrection.

A.) A woman represents "a bride"
B.) The Church is called "A bride"
C.) Seven demons were cast out of her.

Note! I wonder what the Lord is trying to tell us! The church/disciple needs to cast out demons.

Spiritual warfare is geared to take the impurities out of the soul, then the body will heal also. II John 2

Satan has held an advantage over many Christians because of lack of knowledge. For instance there are curses that need to be broken.

Satan is a legal expert give him an inch and he'll take a mile. Curses go back third and fourth generations curses also may come from words spoken of yourself and also spoken against others.

Almost everyone believes in the existence and operation of blessings. But curses are looked upon as something non-existent.

Steps to breaking a curse

1. Acknowledge the area of bondage that you are suffering.
2. Confess all sins, yes even your ancestors sins forgive everyone
3. Renounce all involvements
4. Take authority in Jesus name to break every curse over yourself and your family. Bind any demonic spirits and command them to loose their hold and go to dry places (Luke 11:24).

Spiritual warfare III

God is quite serious when he tells us that we must forgive one another from our hearts. Eph 4:31. 32 Let all bitterness, wrath and anger along with every form of malice be put away from you.

Forgiveness is a choice of their will, not a feeling! Life is full of choices. You make the choice to forgive and the Holy Spirit will be there to assist you!

I remember the time when my next door neighbor's great big Rot-weiler dog came over and bit my little poodle dog when I was gone. My little poodle died.

I admit I was very angry and for days the torment of bitterness troubled me. One day I was painting my house when. The Holy Spirit spoke to me to go over to my neighbor and make amends. At first I discarded the thought but it came back. Finally I put down my paint brush and went over and knocked on their door. His wife answered the door. I asked to see her husband, at that moment she put her hand to her mouth and exclaimed "O' the stress!" When he came to the door I informed him. That I forgave him and that I hoped it wouldn't change our friendship. I went back to my painting and found myself whistling and felt free as a bird. The tormenting of bitterness had gone! Hallelujah!

Jesus Christ the liberator has come to set you free!

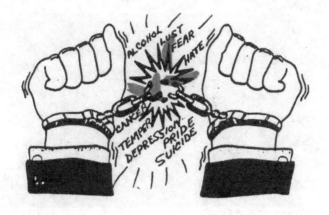

He came to destroy the works of the devil! In order for this to be accomplished, God needs man to declare war on the enemy. To enter spiritual warfare!

Why spiritual warfare?

This question comes up and many Christians don't really understand the purpose of spiritual warfare! Why? Because Satan is a deceiver and he has deceived many in Christendom that Jesus came only to take His people to heaven. Wrong!! Jesus was there when Adam sinned and lost his intimacy with God. We saw the depravity of man the followed, the curses, the evil soul-ties etc. Satan has had a field day. He became the god of this world. (II Cor. 4:4)

The real purpose of Jesus' coming was to restore that which was lost (man's love affair with God). That really cannot be obtained fully until the old nature is replaced with a godly nature. The purpose of spiritual warfare is to learn obedience and attack the enemy driving out all hindrances that stand in the way of man's relationship with God.

Acts 4:13 Now when they saw the boldness of Peter and john they marveled, that these unlearned and ignorant fishermen had been with Jesus. (Results of Jesus' discipleship program!)

The devils strongholds

II Cor. 10:4 Pulling down strongholds. What are some of the devils strongholds?

1. Alcoholism…Families inherit this!
2. Poverty: Generation to generation!
3. Sickness and pain: Cancer, arthritis etc.
4. Female complication: Miscarriages etc.
5. Inability to give and receive love.
6. Marriage breakdowns: Divorce, wife abuse, womanizer etc.
7. Suicide and untimely deaths: family tree.
8. Continued failures: Financial, projects, lower stamp.
9. Gambling: Take on a evil spirit of gambling.
10. Fear of man.
11. Abortion.
12. Drugs.

How to combat this onslaught of the devil. Saturate yourself in the word. (Cleanse your mind.)

A. John 15:3 Now ye are clean thru the word which I have spoken unto you. (Jesus)

B. Eph. 5:26 That he might sanctify and cleanse it with the washing of water by the word.

Spiritual warfare for family

Warfare on behalf of your household
1. Ask forgiveness for yourself- family and your ancestors.
2. Renounce them.
3. Bind the strongman over your house, each individual.
4. Break curses over family, third and fourth generations.
5. Put on armour every day.
6. Pick up cross every day. (Put off and put on) (see sheet)
7. Ask the Father to send his angels to clear out of your house and property all hindering spirits.
8. Learn to "bind and loose." (see sheet)
9. Ask the father to put a hedge of protection around family.

Warfare on behalf of your son

1. Bring him to the throne of grace.
2. Bind the strongman in him.
3. Bind the following!
   A. All deception. (He is deceived)
   B. The spirit of rebellion.
   C. Stubbornness.
   D. Anti-submissiveness
   E. Spirit of witchcraft
      Stubbornness is as the spirit of witchcraft. (Sam. 15:23)
   F. Command suicide spirit to loose its hold on him.

Warfare on behalf of person causing problems
1. Bind the strongman in her.
2. Return all curses back to the sender. (Satan and his cohorts)
3. Make sure you forgive her, bless her. (Luke 6:27, 28)
Vengeance is mine saith the Lord. (Rom. 12:19)

Warfare on behalf of yourselves.

Take authority over all fears-worry-anxieties-apprehension. Command them to loose their hold on you and your family. Cover yourselves with the blood of Jesus.

Matt. 12:29 how can one enter a strongman's house, and spoil his goods, except he first bind the strongman and then spoil his house.

Psalm 97:10 Ye who love the Lord hate evil. (Evil one)

Job 1:10 Satan to God: "You have made a hedge around Job, and his house."

Note! God is no respecter of persons, what He did for Job He will do for you.

Lam. 5:7 Our fathers have sinned and are not, and we have born their iniquities.

Exodus 20:5 Visiting the iniquity of the fathers upon the children unto the third and fourth generation.

Gal. 3:13 Christ has redeemed us form the curse of the law being made a curse for us.

Spiritual Warfare

1. What was the purpose of Jesus' ministry? I John 3:8
2. What is the purpose of Satan's? John 10:10
3. Why spiritual warfare?
4. What is the purpose of acquiring the baptism in the Holy Ghost? Acts 1:8
5. Define discipleship?
6. Where does an unsaved person go when he dies?
7. Where does a saved person go when he dies?
8. How many hell's are there?
9. How many heavens?
10. What is the lake of fire? (Rev. 20:15)
11. Is Satan in charge of Hell? (Matt. 25:41)
12. What is the great white throne judgment? (Rev. 20:11)
13. What is the millennium?
14. Will we know one another in heaven?
15. What happens to a person who doesn't go in the rapture? Can they be saved?
16. According to Rom. 12:2 how are we transformed?
17. Man is made up of three parts. What are they?
18. Define the New Jerusalem. What size will the city be? Compared to the earth?
19. According to Prov. 28:5 What benefit will we receive in seeking the Lord?
20. Where does the word say we are to do the works of Jesus? (John 14:12)
21. Where does it state that the B.H.S. is a separate experience? (Acts 10:44, Acts 9:17)
22. Where does it state that Jesus mentioned "Go and make disciples?"
23. Where does it state that the Israelites are our examples? (I Cor. 10:11)
24. Where does it say "He who does not pick up his cross daily and follow me cannot be my disciple? (Luke 14:27)
25. Where does it say that speaking in tongues is the evidence of the Baptism in the Holy Ghost? 9Acts 10:44-46)

26. Explain why both Joshua and Jesus' names mean salvation?

27. According to I Cor. 1 4.4, what benefit does the person receive in speaking in tongues?

28. According to Psalm 106:15, why did God put "Leanness" into the Israelites souls?

29. According to Psalm 91:14, what benefits are there in "loving the Lord?"

30. According to Matt. 10:1, for what reason did Jesus give the disciples power?

31. According to Luke 9:23-24. How often are we to pick up our cross?

32. What does "Picking up your cross" consist of? (Luke 9:24)

33. According to Luke 10:19, for what reason did Jesus give the disciples power?

34. For what purpose do Christians get baptized by immersion? (Rom. 6:4)

35. According to John 14:15, what is a good sign you love God?

36. According to I John 5:2, what two reasons are given that we know we love the children of God?

37. How does a Christian break a curse?

38. How far back are we to break curses? (Numbers 14:18)

39. How could Jesus be our example, He was without sin?

40. What is the pistol shot that starts the race?

The Reign of the anti-Christ

The reign of the anti-Christ is very near and it's time to focus our attention on what it will be like in that dreadful time. Many of our loved one's are not saved and the tempo of our prayers need to be stepped up.

The mark of the beast is based on a simple decree by anti-Christ: All must accept his mark if they are to buy and sell. Hungry people will enforce the official decree. No one will be allowed to buy food who doesn't have the mark.

Hunger will make beasts out of men. Those who have taken the mark will prey upon those who haven't, taking away their valuables to buy food for themselves.

Hungry people do drastic things. Children will deliver their parents to be killed. Mother's will abandon children. Friends and family will become you enemies. Simply, people will do what they must to survive. In a world pained by hunger, the mark of the beast is an effective way to enforce loyalty to the anti-Christ.

Taking the mark of the beast will seem the only way to survive. That is a lie incorporated in anti-Christ. By taking his mark, a person will not enhance his chances to survive; he will damn his eternal soul. That is the last act of blasphemy the Lord will allow. He will shut the door of grace in the face of them that do.

In refusing the mark you will have to endure a few short days of hunger and pain, but in the end you can save your soul form the pangs of eternal hell.

We are living in a time of grace now, and we need to make every effort to reach our loved one's and spare them for what lies ahead. The choice of taking the mark of the beast or martyrdom should not come to reality. We must obtain a "mind set" that will drive us to our knees in prayer. We need to learn spiritual warfare that will make a difference! We must bind that force of evil that causes us to be passive and have the attributes of being a sluggard! We're at war and God wants you and I to be a winner! We must learn to fight the good fight of faith!

Rev. 13:16-18 Followers of the anti-Christ will receive a mark in their right hand, or in their foreheads. No man will be able to buy or sell without the mark. The mark is the number 666!

Satan: A formidable foe

Although it is true that Satan is a defeated foe, he still has the power to cause many Christians to be hindered in their walk with the Lord. He is a master deceiver, and will take advantage of every opportunity, but thanks to the spiritual warfare program we can be alerted to his methods.

1. I John 4:4 "Greater" is He that is in you than he that is in the world. (Greater is better than great!) The pull of satan is "Great" in this world.

2. Rom. 8:37 We are "more" than conquers through him that loved us. (satan has a lot of Christians conquered.)

3. Luke 11:21, 22 When a "Stronger" than he shall come upon him and over come him. (Stronger is better than strong!) The baptism in the holy spirits is important! "Dunamis" power is needed to fight the enemy!

4. Acts 26:18 Paul:" I was delivered from the power of satan unto God." (We cannot minimize the power of satan!)

5. Luke 4:6 satan to Jesus "All this power I will give you if you will worship me!"

II Cor. 4:4 Satan: The god of this world

I Peter 5:8 Be sober, be vigilant, because your adversary the devil, as a roaring lion, walketh about, seeking whom he may devour.

Satan will hinder you from becoming successful!

1. (I Thess. 2:18) Paul: We would have come unto you but Satan hindered us.

2. (Rom. 15:22) Paul: For which cause I was hindered from coming to you.

3. (I Peter 5:8) Peter: Be sober, be vigilant, because your adversary the devil walks around as a roaring lion, seeking whom he may devour.

4. (Zech. 3:1) Joshua the high priest standing before the angel of the Lord and Satan standing at his right hand to "resist him."

5. (II Cr. 12:7) Paul: Lest I should be exalted above measure, there was given me a thorn in the flesh, a messenger of Satan to buffet me.

Note! Through spiritual warfare, resisting, binding and loosing the child of God is able to overcome the evil one. Luke 11:22 When a stronger than he shall come upon him and overcome him, he taketh from him all his armour, and divided his spoils.

(Ephesians 6:10-18)

To help keep Satan form hindering his walk, the child of God must remember to put on his armour "daily."

1. The helmet of salvation.
2. The breastplate of righteousness.
3. The loins girded with truth.
4. The feet shod with the gospel of peace.
5. Take up the shield of faith.
6. The sword of the word of God.

(Rom. 12:1-16)

I sign my name on my bible every morning. It is my binding word that I will; remember to present your body a living sacrifice each day! Choose each day to serve the lord, obey him, to love him, and to honor him in every thing you do. Choose the fear of the Lord.

Satan's Arrows

The battlefield in spiritual warfare is the mind, (the thought life). When a negative thought comes into your mind you must cast it down. Rebuke it and not accept it. These soldiers of the cross would not submit to the lies of the enemy and therefore were able to carry out the will of the Father.

1. Joshua (Joshua 6:2, 3) The walls of Jericho. "Surely you're not going to do this day after day you'll make a fool out of yourself!"

2. Sarah (Gen. 22:2) To give birth to a baby. "Sarah you are" TOO OLD" to have a baby!"

3. Gideon (Judges 7:10) "Surely your not going to believe you can win with these few men are you!"

4. Moses (Exodus 4:10) "Surely your not going to do that, you can't even talk right!"

5. Abraham (Gen. 2:2) "Surely you're not going to believe God wants you to sacrifice your son do you?"

6. Eve (Gen. 3:1-4) "its o.k. go ahead and eat form the tree. You will not surely die."

7. Jesus (Luke 4:3) "you can turn this stone into bread."

8. Jesus (Matt 26:29) "Jesus, you don't need to go thru with this!! Save yourself" (In the garden of Gethsemane)

9. You "Surely you don't want to do that! Why stick your neck out, you'll be embarrassed!

Note! Take time to seek God. "Lord if this is your will for me then I am willing" "Please give me wisdom and Holy boldness." "I bind all fears" Amen.

Seven duties to your enemies

Matt. 5:44

1. The Christian is to "love them"

2. The Christian is to "Bless them"

3. The Christian is to "do good to them"

4. The Christian is to "Pray for them"

Luke 6:34-36

5. The Christian is to "Lend to them"

6. The Christian is to "Be kind to them"

7. The Christian is to "Be merciful to them"

David, I Sam. 24: 17 David returned good for evil. Stephen, Acts 7:60 Stephen said "Lay not this charge on them." Jesus, Luke 23:34 Forgive them, they don't' know. God, Rom. 5:8 God commended His love toward us in that while we were yet sinners, Jesus Christ died for us.

Samson allowed the enemy to get the best of him. (Like an ox being led to the slaughter) the Philistines poked out his eyes, blinding him, and forced him to grind at the prison house. A laughing stock!

4. Herod (Matt. 14:6)
    Herodias's daughter danced before him in the palace and he was so taken up with lust he told her mother to ask whatever she wanted. She wanted the head of John the Baptist! Herod was sorry but nothing he could do to change it.

II Peter 5:8 "Be sober, be vigilant, because your adversary the devil walks around as a roaring lion seeking whom he may devour."
Psalm 97:10 ye that love the Lord, hate evil.

Prov. 8:13 The fear of the Lord is to hate evil.

Isa. 25:3 Thou will keep him in perfect peace, whose mind is stayed on thee.

II Cor. 10:5 "Casting down imaginations," when a lustful thought comes into your mind, you attack it, you rebuke it, you command it to go in Jesus Name!

Spiritual warfare sexual lust

One of Satan' most powerful weapons is sexual lust. Many great men of God have fallen because of this force of evil. The battlefield is the mind and it needs to be guarded at all times. The soldier of God learns that even though he has power over the enemy, Satan is very deceptive and he needs to be aware of that.

Four great men who fell because of "Lust" for women.
1. David (II Sam. 11:1-4)

    David yielded to the spirit of lust when he saw Bathsheba bathing on the roof next door in the castle. When he looked he allowed his mind to be conceived with that spirit, and therefore drawn to make the wrong decision. (How can two walk together unless they "agree!") David agreed!!

2. Solomon (I Kings 11:1-2)

    Solomon was a victim of the sins of the fathers. He was a womanizer, even though he had many wives. Many strange women caused him to turn to other gods. (Same old story "Man can't handle success!")

3. Samson (Judges 16:4-21)

    Delilah through her persuasive powers was able to cause Samson to yield. Instead of running, (because of pride) he remained.

Signs of a curse

1. Continued poverty.

2. Barrenness and impotency miscarriages- female complications

3. Continued failures projects end up in disaster

4. Untimely and unnatural deaths

5. Sickness and diseases

6. Life traumas: Going from one crisis to another.

7. Mental and emotional breakdown

8. Breakdown in marriages

9. Absence of spiritual power lack of hunger for God's word.

10. Disrespect and disobedience to parents.

See Deut. 28:26-28
Obedience = blessing
Disobedience = curse

Spiritual principles by which curses Operate

1. Prov. 26:2 There is always a cause.

2. Jer. 11:3, 4 Sin opens the door for curses to enter.

3. Mal. 3:8-12 A curse is a spiritual problem and cannot be remedied by natural means.

4. Matt. 18:21-35 In order for a curse to be lifted, the sin root must be removed by obedience and repentance.

5. The law provided no remedy for curses. (Gal. 3:10) (Num.14:18) (Exodus (20:5) (II Sam. 12:10,11 –David) (I Kings 21:29-Ahab)

6. Not until Christ died on the cross can we break the power of the curse (Gal. 3:13).

7. We need to appropriate the provision Jesus made for us just like we need to appropriate our salvation by receiving Jesus Christ as savior. (Matt. 8:16-17)

8. Lam. 5:7 Our Fathers have sinned and are not and we have borne their iniquities.

Curses

Since the sin of Adam the world has drifted away from God. Sin has taken its toll. Curses have come on many families. Take the Kennedy family for instance.

When John Kennedy Jr. died the New York Times carried a lead story, an article titled "The Kennedy curse". It was the latest in along chain or tragedies that has plagued the Kennedy family. Joseph Kennedy was a whisky czar.

1. 1941 Rose Kennedy was institutionalized (Mentally ill) still there.
2. 1944 Joseph P. Kennedy Jr. (oldest son) died plane crash (World War II)
3. 1948 Kathleen Kennedy died in plane crash (28 years old)
4. 1963 Patrick Kennedy (2nd son of President Kennedy) died after two days of life.
5. 1963 Nov. 23rd John F. Kennedy was assassinated (46 years old)
6. 1964 Senator Edward Kennedy escapes death in a plane crash.
7. 1968 Robert Kennedy was assassinated (June 5th)
8. 1969 Edward Kennedy drove off a bridge after a party in Chappaquiddick.
9. 1973 Edward Kennedy's son (Edward Jr.) lost right leg (cancer)
10. 1973 Joseph P. Kennedy II (Son of Robert and Ethel Kennedy) is killed in a driving accident.
11. 1984 David Kennedy (Son of Robert and Ethel Kennedy) is killed in a driving accident.
11. 1984 David Kennedy (Son of Robert Kennedy) dies of a drug overdose.
12. 1986 Patrick Kennedy (teenage son of Edward Kennedy) cocaine addiction
13. 1991 William Kennedy Smith was accused of raping a woman (tried and acquitted)"
14. 1997 Michael Kennedy (son of Robert Kennedy) died in a skiing accident.

Christian: God is calling you into battle!

It doesn't take long (if a Christian has the desire to go all the way with the Lord) to realize that the Bible is a "**Book of warfare.**" That God has a calling on his life to be a soldier. **A soldier because there's a war on,** there's an enemy that needs to be defeated.

II Tim. 2:4 No man that warreth entangles himself with the affairs of this world; that he may please him who hath "**Chosen him to be a soldier.**

II Tim. 2:3 Endure hardness as a **good soldier of Jesus Christ**.

II Tim. 3:12 Yea, and all that will live godly in Christ Jesus **shall suffer persecution**!

John 15:20 If they persecuted me, **they will also** persecute you!

Matt. 10:20 Ye **shall be hated** for my name's sake, but he that endureth till the end, shall be saved.

Exodus 15:3 The Lord is a man of **war**!

I Peter 5:8 **Be sober, be vigilant**, because your enemy as a roaring lion, walketh about seeking whom he may devour.

Eph. 6:11 **Put on the whole armour of God**, that ye ay be able to stand against the wiles of the devil.

Eph. 6:12 For we "**wrestle**" not against flesh and blood, but against principalities, powers, against the rulers of darkness of this world, against spiritual wickedness in high places.

I Peter 4:12, 13 Beloved, think it not strange concerning the fiery trial which is to try you, but rejoice in as much as ye are **partakers of Christ's sufferings**; that when his Glory shall be revealed, ye may be glad with exceeding joy.

Psalm 144:1 Blessed be the lord my strength, which teaches my hands to **war** and my fingers **to fight**!

John 14:12 (Jesus) verily, I say unto you, the works that I do **ye shall do also**. (Have compassion-cast out devils-heal the sick).

Soul Ties

The soul of man plays an important role in regards to the communion we have with the Lord. As we read God's word we learn:

1. Deut. 4:29 We seek the Lord with our soul.
2. Deut. 6:5 We Love the Lord with our soul.
3. Deut. 10:12 We Serve the Lord with our soul.
4. Deut. 11:18 We Store God's word with our soul.
5. Deut. 30:10 We obey God's word with our soul.
6. Prov. 19:8 We receive God's wisdom with our soul.
7. Psalm 142:7 We praise the lord with our soul.
8. Luke 1:46 We magnify the Lord with our soul.
9. Isa. 26:9 We desire the Lord with our soul.

Cleave-clave-knit-joined

Good soul-ties
1. Gen. 2:24 (Husband and wife) a man shall leave his father and mother and "cleave" to his wife.
2. Joshua 23:8 (Believer/God) "Cleave" unto the Lord your God.
3. I Sam. 18:1 9Between friends) David and Jonathan's souls were "knit together."
4. Col. 2:2, 19 (Believers/Congregations) souls "knit together" in love.
5. II Sam. 20:2 9Believer/ leader) the men of Judah "clave" to their king.

Evil soul-Ties
1. Gen. 34:1-3 (Thru Fornication) Schechem's soul "Clave" to Dinah's soul.
2. I Kings 11:2 Solomon "clave" unto strange women.
3. Joshua 23:12,13 (Believer/ world) if you go back and "cleave" unto these nations your God will no more drive out the enemy before you.

Soul-ties play an important part of a person being set free. Satan has had his way and does not give up easily. He knows his legal rights and only when the Child of God confesses his involvement and renounces them, can he break the bondage. If every there was any affiliation with the following, there must be a breaking of respective soul-ties.

1. False religions = Jehovah witnesses occultism-Moonies etc.
2. Martial arts = When connected to Easter Religion.
3. Horoscopes-witchcrafts hypnotist

Love the Lord – Hate evil

In the spiritual war that is taking place in this world today that Christian is facing an enemy that is very deceitful. Satan has had a lot of victories because Christians have missed the boat in this loving the Lord bit.

Every action has a counter part of reaction and a person cannot really love the Lord until he has a hatred for the devil. A person needs to take a look at the damage the enemy has done to many families. He has battered them from pillar to post due to the sins of the fathers that has given him legal rights to bring on the curses and depravity.

As the Christian matures there will be two reasons that motivate him. 1. His love for the Lord. 2. His hatred for the devil. Success will come no other way.

1. Psalm 97:10 Ye that love the Lord, hate evil. (Evil one)
2. Prov. 8:13 Fear of the Lord is to hate evil.
3. Psalm 111:10 Fear of the Lord is the beginning of wisdom.
4. Rom. 12:9 Love without hypocrisy. Abhor that which is evil. Cleave to that which is good.
5. Amos 5:15 Hate evil – love the good.
6. I John 2:15 Love not the world.

Jesus our example

Our Lord Jesus was loving and compassionate man, but there were times that he had a righteous anger like that time in the temple. He overturned that tables of the money changers.

1. John 2:12-16 Jesus chased the money changers out of the temple using a whip with small cords, he drove them out.

2. Matt. 23:27 Jesus: Woe to you Pharisees! Woe to you scribes! "Hypocrites", white sepulchres "generations of vipers!"

Heb 1:2 God, in these last days hath spoken to us <u>by His Son.</u>

Matt 11:29 Take my yoke upon you and <u>Learn of me.</u>

Good news!! Jesus Christ has given the Church power to bind the enemy and obtain victory in every situation!!

Model prayer for breaking curses
(To be read aloud)

Heavenly Father, in the name of Jesus, I am truly your child. I have been purchased by the blood of Jesus. I belong to you. I do not belong to the devil. The devil has no right to me and no power over me because of the precious blood of Jesus.

Father, you have known all my sins. I confess them all to you. I repent of them now. I ask you to forgive me. Forgive me of every sin and remove the stains out of my heart and my life for your word tells me when I confess my sins, you will forgive me and cleanse me from all unrighteousness. I not only confess my own sins, but also the sins of my parents, Grandparents and Great-grandparents-sins which brought curses into my family. I confess those sins to you that the power of curse might be broken through the shed blood of Lord Jesus Christ.

In the name of Jesus, I now rebuke, break and loose myself and my family from my own sins, the sins of my ancestors or from any other person. I am redeemed by the blood of the Lamb, therefore I am redeemed from the curse of the law. I break the power of every spoken curse of every evil that came out of my own mouth. I take back all the ground I ever yielded to the devil and establish myself in faith in the Lord Jesus Christ and claim the blessing rather than the curse. I break the power of every evil word that was knowingly or unknowingly spoken against me by any other person. I cancel that spoken word and the power of the curse in the authority of the name of Jesus Christ.

I believe in your power, Lord Jesus. I believe in your redemption. I believe in my heart you are my savior – you are my deliverer. I confess you with my mouth and I confess that the power of every curse is now broken in the authority of your name.

I command every spirit which has come in through the door of curse to leave me now, in the name of Jesus Christ. Amen

Note! There were thousands of Jews living in Spain in the late 1400's. In 1492, the year Columbus sailed to America, King Ferdinand

and Queen Isabella signed and official decree expelling all Jews from Spain. Spain was a great nation. Her empire extended far and wide, however, Spain began to decline, and her empire disintegrated.

Spain has never returned politically, economically or culturally to her former glory and is today considered one of the poorest nations in Western Europe. Also considered one of the driest in the spiritual realm.

Could it be God's law? "I will bless those who bless you (Israelites) and those who curse you will be cursed." (Gen. 12:3)

God: War minded?

The word of God informs us that there are two forces in the spiritual realm that are out to destroy one another.

God vs. Satan

John 10:10 The devil comes to steal, kill and <u>destroy</u>.
I John 3:8 Jesus came to <u>destroy</u> the works of the devil.

After the Israelites were liberated from bondage in Egypt, God state: "The Lord is a man of war" (Exodus 15:3) meaning that the Promised Land (The land of the Hitities, Hivities, the Persites, the Canaanites etc.) is theirs, but they would need to fight for every foot of it! Cast them out! (Deut. 7:1)

Prov. 6:6 The word says "consider the ant- consider her ways" the ant is persistent, yes, but it is considered on of the most vicious fighters in the world also!

II Tim. 2:4 The Christian is called to be a soldier.

Acts 1:8 you shall receive "Power" after the Holy Ghost is come upon you. (Why? Because you need power to win a war!)

II Tim 3:12 Yea, and all that will live godly in Christ Jesus shall suffer persecution.

Eph. 6:13 We are instructed to put on our armor. Why? Because the enemy's arrows are coming at you. (There's a war on!)

Psalm 69:18 Draw nigh unto my soul, and redeem it, deliver me <u>because of my enemies.</u>

Psalm 27:11 Teach me thy way O' Lord, and lead in a lain path, <u>because of my enemies.</u>

Prov. 20:18 Every purpose is established by counsel: and with good advice make war!!

Matt. 28:19 God ye there fore and make disciples. (Soldiers)

Note! Jesus Christ did not come just to take man to heaven, but to build an army with the power of righteousness, having a righteous anger against the powers of darkness.

Matt. 21:12 Jesus took a whip and chased the moneychangers out of the temple, overturning their tables, yet, Jesus was sinless. A man with righteous anger, yet loving. (John 2:15) Psalm 97:10 Ye that love the Lord, hate evil!! (Evil one).

Good Morning Lord!

I give thanks unto thee heavenly Father thru Jesus Christ thy dear Son for the protection during the night for myself and my family.

(Say out Loud) (Joshua 24:15)

I choose this day to serve you, to obey you, to seek you face, to love you, to honor you and to worship you. I choose the fear of the Lord. (Prov. 1:29)

I put on my armor. (Piece by piece) (Eph. 6:13-17)

The helmet of salvation – the breastplate of righteousness. My loins girded with truth—feet shod with the preparation of the Gospel of peace—I take up the shield of faith and the sword of the word of God. (In Jesus name)

SOLDIER OF GOD

Did you put on your
ARMOUR TODAY!

EPHESIANS 6: 13-17

1. The Helmet of Salvation.
2. The Breastplate of Righteousness.
3. The Loins girded with Truth.
4. The Feet shod with the preparation of the Gospel of Peace.
5. The Shield of Faith.
6. The Sword of the Word of God.

I pick up my cross and die to the old nature. (Luke 9:23-24)
    1. I put off selfishness—I put on agape love.
    2. I put off fear—I put on courage and holy boldness.
    3. I put off lust—I put on righteousness and purity.
    4. I put off all lying, anger, wrath, blasphemy and filthy communication—I put on kindness, meekness, humility and longsuffering. (Eph. 4:20-27)

I present my body a living sacrifice. (Rom. 12:1, 9-21)
    1. I will not be conformed to this world.
    2. I will love without hypocrisy.
    3. I will cleave to that which is good.
    4. I will be kindly affectionate one to another.
    5. I will not be slothful in business.
    6. I will be fervent in spirit.
    7. I will rejoice in the hope of the Lord.
    8. I will be patient in tribulation.
    9. Continuing instant in prayer.
    10. Helping the saints.
    11. I will bless them that persecute me.
    12. I will rejoice with them that rejoice.
    13. I will weep with them that weep.
    14. I will not pay back evil for evil.
    15. When my enemy hungers, I will feed him.
    16. I will overcome evil with good.

Note! Life is full of choices! Choose to serve God each day.

There are many families that are going thru the same circumstances because of sins committed (as far back as four generations) that brought on curses that has plagued them. But! We have good news!! Jesus Christ came to restore us!! He became a curse for us on the cross and now we have the power to break every curse! We need to repent and ask the Lord to forgive ourselves, our family and our ancestors for sins committed, to renounce them and then break the curses.

Isn't it strange?

That Mary Magdalene was the first to see Jesus after His resurrection!

1. A woman represents a bride (The Church).
2. Seven demons were cast out of her. (Old Adamic nature).

Isn't it strange?
That Joshua and Jesus' names both mean salvation (Jehoshua)

1. Joshua drove out the "nations." (Hitites-Hivites-Canaanites-Armorites etc.)

2. Jesus drove out the "Old Nature"

3. The Church is empowered also to do the same. To drive out the "Old Nature" (Fear-lust-pride-hate-worry-rejection-etc.)

"Fear"

If there is one weapon Satan has, to keep the Christian soldier off balance, it is fear. When fear dominates a Christian's mind, Faith seems to diminish. (I John 4:18 Fear hath torment.)

Take the great man of God Elijah, even after his tremendous victory at Mount Carmel he fled in fear when Jezebel threatened him. It can happen to you too!

There are two kinds of fear mentioned in the Bible:
1. Phobias Fear (5399) Is the most common, it is found 46 times in the New Testament. Webster's Dictionary = (To be frightened or intimidated by something.)

2. Deilos Fear (1169) is a deadly kind of fear. It is found 5 times in the New Testament. (Faithless-Timid-Fearful)

> A. Rev. 21:8 But the fearful, unbelieving, whore mongers, murders etc.
> B. II Tim. 1:7 God hath not given you a spirit of fear, but power, love and a sound mind.
> C. John 14:27 Let not your heart be troubled, neither let it be afraid.
> D. Matt. 8:26 Jesus: "Why are you so fearful?"
> E. Mark 4:40 Jesus: "Why are you so fearful?"

How to combat fear
II Tim. 1:7 For God has not given to us a spirit of fear, but of
1. Power
2. Love
3. A sound mind.

1. Power = Dunamis (1411 Strong's): It is important that a Christian receive the baptism in the Holy Ghost! This power is needed to be set free.

2. Love = (Agape Love): It is important that a Christian love the Lord, but also to hate the devil. Psalm 97:10 Ye that love the Lord, hate evil. There are three kinds of love: Agape, Plileo, Eros.

3. Sound Mind = Healing of the soul. (The thrust of Jesus' ministry) Soul=Mind, will and the emotions.

Always go to the root of the problem. How did Satan gain legal rights? It could be that you inherited it from your ancestors. It could be from some experiences you've encountered yourself. Seek the Lord! Confess your fear as sin, your own sin, your family's sins and the sins of your ancestors that would open any doors. Renounce them. Now that you have taken back all legal rights of the enemy, break all curses as far back as third and fourth generations that would bring bondage in this area. Take authority in Jesus name and command Satan to loose his hold on you.

FEAR II

God said 366 times "Fear Not" Sin brought on fear (Gen. 3:10) Adam: "I was afraid!" Fear can keep a believer from maturity! It is a big tool of the devil, even for the spiritual giants!

What are the effects of insecurity?

1. Fear of oneself Afraid you cannot do the job you get called on and get paralyzed with fear.

2. Fear of others: This comes from the seed we inherited from Adam. (Adam became afraid of God) (Afraid of others) Prov. 29:25 Fear of man bringeth a snare.

3. Fear of decision: One of the greatest problems in America are men indecision, who can't take authority in the home as fathers and husbands. Matt. 25: 24-26 Parable of the talents. The one with the one talent said "I was afraid!" What did his master say? "Thou wicked and slothful servant!" Fear produces what has an appearance of laziness!

4. Fear of failure: Fear paralyzes many so badly they will not attempt anything.

How to cope with fear

1. We need to recognize that our battle ground against fear is in the mind. What controls our thoughts, controls us. That's why Paul states (Col. 3:1, 2) seek those things which are above, set your affections on the things above. Isa. 26:3 "He will give perfect peace whose mind is stayed on thee"

2. Fear is often an outward manifestation of inner guilt. I John 3:21 Beloved if our heart condemn us not, then we have confidence toward God.

3. Stay busy: Inactivity often leads to an unhealthy introspection which brings on low self esteem, then guilt, then fear. Activity and plain physical exercise can help.

4. It could be caused by an evil spirit:
    If it is caused by the struggle against the flesh rather than a demon it will improve with prayer.

I John 4:18 Perfect love casteth out fear. (Our love affair with the Lord)

Warfare Language against demons

As we look into the scriptures we see that the entire Bible is a book of warfare.

In battling with the demon powers of hell, God has provided us with the ammunition to win every confrontation with the word.

Jesus set the example for us when he was confronted by Satan. He answered him "It is written."

In the Psalms and other books of the Bible there is a warfare language that can be used with effectiveness. Here are some of them.

1. Psalm 59:10 God shall let me see my desire on my enemies.
2. Psalm 140:10 Let burning coals fall on this demons head.
3. Psalm 70:02, Psalm 109:2 Spin confusion on demons.
4. Psalm 58:07 Cut demons to pieces.
5. Psalm 18:13 Hail stones, coals of fire, shoot out lightning.
6. Psalm 35:06 Dark and slippery is your path.
7. Psalm 109:17 Return curses back to the sender.
8. Psalm 144:06 Shoot arrows at them.
9. Psalm 58:06 Break their teeth.
10. Psalm 35:05 Let the angel of the Lord chase them.
11. Psalm 35:05 Let the angel of the persecute them.
12. Psalm 10:15 Break arm of demons.
13. Psalm 11:06 Rain snares, fire, and brimstone on demons.
14. II Kings 9:36 Loose the hounds of heaven on Jezebel.
15. Isaiah 4:04 Loose spirit of burning and judgment on demons.
16. Ezekiel 38:04. Hooks in the jaws.
17. Jer. 51:53 Ask the Lord to send spoilers.
18. Psalm 18:14 Stick arrows in them.
19. Psalm 35:08 Loose destruction on them.
20. Exodus 23:28 Ask the father to send the hornets of the lord on them.
21. Heb. 4:13 Read this to the demons if they are hiding.
22. Heb. 1:07, 14 Ask the Father to send His angels to assist.

23. Gen. 3:24 Ask the Father to send angels with their flaming swords.
24. Isa. 62:07 Give them no rest.
25. Daniel 3:29 Cut them up in pieces.
26. Phil. 2:09-11 Remind demons that at the name of Jesus every knee shall bow and every tongue will confess that Jesus Christ is Lord.

Remind demons that we are approaching him from our position in the heaven-lies with Christ Jesus. Eph. 2:6 (3rd heaven).

It is important to remember that you do not send the angels, but ask the Father to send them. Jesus told Peter that he could of asked the Father to send them. (Matt. 26:52, 53).

Why would God call:
"David"
"A man after God's own heart"
(Acts 13:22)

I Samuel 16:18

A. Cunning (skillful) in playing.

B. A mighty valiant (brave) man.

C. A MAN OF WAR!

D. Prudent (Wisdom-caution) in matters.

E. A comely (Attractive) person.

I Samuel 17:20

A. Obeyed his father (Jesse)

B. Had respect for God's anointed. (Saul) (I Samuel 24:6)

C. He gave the Lord the credit. (I Sam. 17:47)

D. Behaved himself wisely. (I Sam. 18:5, 14, 15)
   (Having knowledge-good judgment)

E. His love for the Lord all through the Psalms (his praise-his up-his downs but never losing his love for God)

F. David's confession of sin. (Psalm 51) II Sam. 2:13 David: "I have sinned against the Lord."

Anger

If there is one thing that will stunt the Christian growth in a disciple, it is un-forgiveness. A disciple must search his heart to see if there is ay wicked way in him.

Psalm 26:2 Examine me, O' Lord and prove me; try my reigns and my heart.

Think back on your life, was there a time when you lost your temper? Was there a time when you hated someone? Was there a time when you were insanely jealous? Etc.

1. Rom 12:14 Bless them that persecute you; bless and curse not.

2. Luke 6:27 But I say unto you, love your enemies. Do good to them that hate you!

3. Luke 6:28 Bless them that curse you, pray for them which despitefully use you!

4. Luke 6:35 love your enemies and do good and lend, hoping for nothing again and your reward shall be great. Ye shall be the children of the highest.

5. Rom. 12:16 Recompense to no man evil for evil. (Pay back) Rom. 12:19 Vengeance is mine saith the Lord!

6. Matt. 18:21 If you forgive men their trespasses your heavenly will also forgive you. But if you don't forgive them your heavenly Father will not forgive you.

7. Mat. 5:23 If you bring your gift to the altar and you remember that your brother hath ought against you, leave your gift at the altar and go see if you can reconcile with him.

8. Rom. 12:20 Therefore if your enemy hungers, feed him! If he's thirsty, give him drink, heap coals of fire on his head.

9. Matt 18:21 Because you will not forgive, God will send the tormentors. (demons)

10. Matt. 5:20 For I say unto you. That except your righteousness shall exceed the righteousness of the scribes and the Pharisees, ye shall in no way enter the kingdom of heaven!

Conclusion

Thank you for reading my book! Like I stated at the beginning I am frustrated why so many Christians are having problems. This book is not the "cut and dried formula" but I hope it will open up your eyes into the heart of Jesus Christ and hear His still small voice!

God bless you!

Contact Len Ward
P.O Box 1024
Superior, WI 54880

Home (715) 392-4330
Cell (218) 428-2291
Email LenHWard@msn.com

Psalms 144:15 Happy are those people, whose God is the Lord.